Complete Handbook of

Kindergarten Music Lesson Plans

and Activities

Complete Handbook of
Kindergarten Music Lesson Plans
and Activities

Marcelle Vernazza

Parker Publishing Company, Inc.   West Nyack, New York

Library of Congress Cataloging in Publication Data

Vernazza, Marcelle.
  Complete handbook of kindergarten music lesson
plans and activities.

  Includes index.
  1. Kindergarten—Music.   2. School music—
Instruction and study—United States.   I. Title.
MT920.V37   372.8'7044   80-39724
ISBN 0-13-161190-9

Printed in the United States of America

Dedication

To my husband, Jerome, who listened and pondered over the children's music; to Ben, who liked the drum the best; and to Martha, who sang her way through kindergarten.

Previous Book

Treasury of American Music Lesson Plans

How to Use This Complete Kindergarten Music Program

This book, written for kindergarten teachers, presents a comprehensive music program for kindergarten children. Using these practical easy-to-follow lesson plans, the teacher will be able to develop every facet of music in the classroom. All lessons take into consideration the natural musical abilities and interests of young children as well as the physical, social, emotional, and mental growth patterns of the kindergarten age.

Each lesson plan sets the stage, notes the materials needed, outlines the lesson sequence, and, in some cases, provides the dialogue for the teacher (printed in italics). It focuses on specific elements of music, incorporating abilities and information already acquired by the children. Although each lesson plan is presented in detailed sequence, the teacher will find it easy to enlarge upon the lesson or adapt it to a specific situation, problem, or child.

The lessons are designed to develop children's musical skills and build a large repertoire of musical experiences. Teachers will find lessons to teach songs for many occasions, basic rhythmic movements and their variations, games and dances, lessons that tell musical stories and inspire dramatic play, and lessons to encourage instrumental exploration and beginning instruction on drums, bells, and keyboard. These lessons are designed to help children perform to please themselves, other children, their families, and, occasionally, a formal audience.

There are lessons to orient children to a new group situation, lessons to develop individual musical abilities, lessons with opportunities for sensory participation, to undergird other arts, to

7

enhance the learning of daily living skills, to take children into the world of fantasy, to stimulate them to work or to relax them after strenuous activity. In fact, these lessons will enable the kindergarten teacher to establish a total musical environment in which children flourish.

Lessons in *Part 1* encourage free exploration of movement directed toward developing basic rhythm concepts. The lessons deal with gross body and limb rhythms, and move gradually to fine finger and toe movements.

The lessons in vocal responses emphasize original and patterned chants and simple pentatonic songs using easy and natural progressions such as descending minor thirds (so-mi) and rising triad intervals (do-mi and sol-do). There are songs to establish moods, express individual feelings and tell about everyday happenings, songs to celebrate joyous occasions and songs to supply and stimulate a sense of humor.

Part 2 is made up of progressive lessons using drums generally available in kindergartens. In a sequence of developing rhythm concepts the lessons take the children from the simplest flat hand motions through a development of left-right and hand-finger coordination.

Rhythmic speech and other vocal responses, as well as foot and body movements, appear in rhymes, song stories, games and dramatizations.

Part 3 contains lessons using the kinds of bells that intrigue kindergarteners. These are bells that jingle or ring, bells that are struck with mallets, cymbal bells, and various other large and small bells. Opportunities for exploration are given and correct playing techniques are incorporated into the lesson plans.

Part 4 focuses on first keyboard experiences. Any available keyboard(s) may be used. The lessons progress through an introductory keyboard program oriented toward becoming completely familiar with the topography of the keyboard and with producing simple music on it. No steps are left out as the lessons move slowly and easily in a developmental pattern. The lessons include attractive rhymes, chants and songs.

The visual aspects of the keyboard as well as the range of pitches and the percussive, melodic and harmonic potentials of the keyboard are combined with the development of hand, finger, and eye coordination and right and left hand skills. After each presentation the teacher will find the children anxious to use the newly learned skills as a basis for further independent practice at the keyboard.

The lessons in *Part 5* combine the various areas of musical performance and invite use of the children's developing musical skills and natural aptitude for improvisation.

Music for special days, times and seasons is the basis for culminating activities and programs. Practical models have been developed from the activities in this book. These models will help the teacher plan programs that are a natural part of the learning process.

Being part of an audience and listening to many kinds of music are important parts of kindergarten music. In Part Five there are models for demonstration lessons and suggestions for programs to be given for children.

This handbook of practical, yet creative, ready-to-use lesson plans presents a self-contained kindergarten music program which all kindergarten teachers with or without special music training can use.

THE MUSICAL NATURE OF
KINDERGARTEN CHILDREN

Young children are natural and enthusiastic as they move, chant and sing, and explore sound makers.

Some characteristic rhythmic movements of these children are walking, running, jumping, hopping, stamping, galloping, rolling and crawling, twisting and turning, and stretching and bending. Their spontaneous movements assume rhythm when repeated. When children move at random, pleasurable patterns evolve, sometimes with matching song fragments. Often such patterns develop into extemporaneous dances. No rhythm is too complicated as long as young children feel a dynamic pulse.

Rhythmic combinations begin to appear after children feel secure in single rhythms. A run, then a jump; a gallop around a circle; a walk with a sudden stop; a twirl followed by a collapse on the floor —these and many more such combinations please the moving child. Their imitations of animals, people, imagined creatures or machines also develop combinations of basic movements.

Young children sing much the same way they talk—freely and easily. They imitate what they hear. They experiment with original musical phrases. They improvise rambling ballads, the melody wandering up and down without any discernible plan. Sometimes children sing simply because they like the sound of their voice and are intrigued with their own success. Their chants generally describe the work or play in which they are involved or a strong feeling they have about a person or an immediate situation.

Natural styles and abilities vary, and singing skills are yet to be developed. At first children may be more interested in producing words and sounds for their own sake than in following conventional melodies. They are apt to sing softly to themselves if they are occupied with a task they enjoy. Most children develop a special song fragment or "Happy Song" which they hum or sing when they are at peace with the world. In a group they sing more forcefully, although a few children may refrain from singing with others until they feel completely confident of themselves.

Children are attracted to many kinds of sounds and like to clap hands, pat knees, stamp feet, and create mouth sounds. They also like to experiment with objects that produce sharp or ringing sounds. Pleasurable ways they produce sounds are slapping a table top, hitting a drum or other resonating object, shaking a bell, blowing a whistle, scraping rough surfaces together. Rarely satisfied with making a sound only once, children repeat sounds and make them into rhythm patterns, sometimes in conjunction with singing and/or moving.

The musical play of young children is often quite dramatic. Like their games, music becomes a practice period or a recreation of recent experiences. They are interested in imitating what they see and hear and in playing roles from their own experiences. Melody offers more variety than speech; dance is more stimulating than a walk; sounds they create themselves are more interesting than those other people make. Their dramatic play combines movement and singing and is enhanced with the manipulation of simple sound makers or reinforced by music they hear.

With these musical abilities and interests of kindergarten children, kindergarten teachers can work to develop musicianship and musical skills, and build a repertoire of musical experiences that children can take with them as they grow and develop.

Marcelle Vernazza

Contents

11

Part 4
Activities for Keyboard—159

Part 5
Special Activities and Programs—187

Index—233

Complete Handbook of
Kindergarten Music Lesson Plans
and Activities

PART 1

Activities for Singing & Moving to Music

Part 1

ACTIVITIES FOR SINGING AND MOVING TO MUSIC

17

♪ ♪ ♪ ♪ ♪

PART ONE focuses on the beginnings of kindergarten musicianship—chanting, singing, moving, and listening to music. The first activities deal with the exploration of sounds children make themselves and sounds they hear in their immediate environment.

Some activities deal with chants, the rhythmic bridge between speech and song. Chants and songs are important in the music learning sequence, and children enjoy them. Their first interest is the word content, then the rhythm, finally the melody. The songs in Part One are the first of many to follow. The more simple songs children sing, the better singers they become.

Rhythmic activities begin with exploration of body language, natural large body movements in rhythm. One-step movements (walking, running, jumping) follow. Then come galloping, skipping and other step combinations. Activities in imitative and free rhythms are designed to be the natural outgrowth of the basic rhythms.

As children listen to music, be it solo piano, brass band, symphony, or pop group, they pick up the rhythm and the mood. Compositions suggested here have strong rhythms or suggest particular moods. All activities are part of a wide-based beginning repertoire.

Exploring Sounds

MAKING A CLAPPING CHAIN

Materials

Tape recorder

Pre-planning

- Explore ways to clap and note the differences in the resulting sounds (full hands, palm on palm, fingers on palm, fingers, cupped hands).
- Check the tape recorder.

Musical Focus

- Awareness of hand clapping sounds
- Organization of clapping patterns into a sound chain

Activities and Directions

- *Clapping is a good way to show how much we enjoy ourselves.*
- Lead informal clapping. Note the ways the children clap.
- *There are different ways to clap. Here is one way. Clap palms together. This is a loud clap.* The children clap.
- Clap fingers together. Note that this is a soft clap. The children do the finger clapping.
- *Let's make a clapping chain. Each one of you will have a turn to clap the way you want to.*
- (Record this.) The children, in quick succession, demonstrate their clapping.
- *Were all the claps alike?* Have the children talk about how they clapped.
- *Listen to our clapping chain.* (Play back the tape.)
- Discuss the loudness and softness of the claps and other differences.
- *We can make different sounds when we clap.*

Continuing Lessons

- Make other sound chains using sounds made by the feet, the mouth, and a combination of original sounds.
- Relate this lesson to "We Laugh at the Clowns."

THE SONG WE KNOW THE BEST

Pre-planning

- Select a very familiar song.
- Review the rhythm of the song by clapping out the words as you sing.

Musical Focus

- Discriminating listening
- Developing the concept of words, melody, and rhythm belonging together

Activities and Directions

- *Sometimes we clap while we sing.*
- Sing the familiar song and lightly clap the rhythm of the words.
- Have the children sing and clap the song. Emphasize light clapping.
- *I am going to clap one phrase (part) of the song. Listen carefully, then raise your hand if you can sing it to me.*
- After one child sings it, have everyone repeat it.
- Sing another phrase. Children guess, then sing it.
- Have volunteers clap phrases of the song for others to guess and sing.
- Everyone sings the song, clapping as they sing.
- *Our clapping kept the rhythm of the words and melody.*

Continuing Lessons

- Repeat the lesson with other familiar songs.

- For a more demanding lesson, clap the rhythm of a familiar song without singing the words. Have the children guess the song.

SOUNDS OF ZOO CREATURES

Materials

- Chart paper, felt pen
- (Optional) Pictures of zoo animals

Musical Focus

- Characteristics of creature sounds (high-low, loud-soft, squeaky-roaring, etc.)
- Arranging sounds into a sequence

Other Learning

- Awareness of mouth sounds
- Recognizing printed names of zoo creatures

Activities and Directions

- *The animals at the zoo make different kinds of sounds.*
- Print "lion" at the top of the chart paper.
- *What kind of sound does a lion make?* (loud-roar)
- *What other creatures live in the zoo?* (Show pictures.)
- Print the names of suggested animals on the chart paper.
- Go through the list of names as volunteers make appropriate sounds.
- Discuss the characteristics of the sounds.
- Have each child choose a creature to imitate.
- In quick succession each child makes the sound of the chosen creature.
- *Let's all make the animal sounds at once like a chorus of animals.*

Continuing Lessons

- Combine this lesson with "Animals at the Zoo."

- Have a zoo parade with sounds on the way to the playground. Add a light drum beat for background to the parade.
- Use the same ideas to explore sounds of farm animals, machines, and sounds at home or school.

THE BIRD RONDO

| | A | bird | is | sing - ing, | Lis - ten | to | it | sing. |
| *(Last time)* | The | birds | are | sing - ing, | Lis - ten | to | them | sing. |

Pre-planning

- In rondo form one-part (A) returns between each new part (A B A C A D A, etc.). Parts may have descriptive names such as (A) all the birds, (B) Susan bird, etc.

Musical Focus

- Form in music—the concept of sound organization
- Making musical mouth sounds

Activities and Directions

- *Did you ever hear a bird singing?*
- *What did it sound like?* (Chirp, tweet, whistle)
- *This is the first part of "The Bird Rondo." Sing it.*
- Sing it with the children two or three times.
- *Let's make up some bird songs.* Ask for volunteers.
- In between the volunteer bird songs, everyone sings the (A) or "all the birds" part.
- End the rondo with all the birds singing together (last verse).
- *"The Bird Rondo" has one part we sing in between the different parts.*

Continuing lessons

- Outline the form of the song on chart paper, using children's names or colors to name the parts.
- Add finger cymbals to the (A) part.

WE LAUGH AT THE CLOWNS
(Developing a Sound Chain)

Materials

- Tape recorder (cassette or reel-to-reel)
- (Optional) Picture(s) of clowns

Pre-planning

- Perfect your skill in using the tape recorder.

Musical Focus

- Developing careful listening with laughter
- Sequencing sounds
- Experiencing natural physical reactions to rhythmic chanting

Other Learning

- Introduction to the tape recorder
- Taking turns

Activities and Directions

- (chant) *When we're at the circus we laugh at the clowns. They are the funniest people in town.*
- Repeat the chant with the children until they feel the accents. Encourage natural rhythmic movement such as swaying or soft foot tapping.
- Discuss clowns. (Show the pictures.) *Who has seen a real clown? What is funny about clowns? Do clowns make you laugh?*
- Show me how you laugh. (Record this.) Children laugh together, then one at a time.

- Play back the tape for the children.
- *Let's plan our laughs in a different order.* Work out a sequence with the children or, to make it easier, point to every other child in time for him/her to laugh.
- *Let's record our funny chant and our laughing together and then one at a time.* Record.
- Play back the tape.
- Discuss the tape—the order of the laughs, the clarity of the chant, the kinds of laughs.
- *Laughing is a musical sound. Putting together laughs is like putting together little melodies. We made a sound chain of happy laughs.*

Continuing Lessons

- Develop other sound chains of clapping, spoken names, contrasting available sounds.

Chants

SEE THE BUS

See the *bus* up *on* the *street,*
Let's get *on* and *rest* our *feet.*
If the *bus* rolls *down* the *hill,*
Will you *to* pay *the bill?*

Musical Focus

- Awareness of the even beat
- Developing the ability to chant (to speak with inflection in rhythm)

Other Learning

- Developing coordination of hands, head and voice

Activities and Directions

- *Let's clap an even beat together.*
- After establishing the beat, say the chant for the children.
- Repeat it with the children several times.
- Chant without clapping (to check the words and rhythm).
- Chant and slap thighs (patsch).
- Chant and move head in rhythm.
- Combine chanting, clapping or slapping and moving the head.
- *Your voice, your hands, and your head all kept time together.*

Continuing Lessons

- Use the lesson with playground chants contributed by the children.
- *Rolling down the street on my roller skates,*
  Left foot, right foot, roller skates.
  If I fall and skin my shin,

26

Mamma, poppa, everyone will know where I've been.
(Pretend skating. Start on the *left* foot.)
- Activity for the playground (with or without a winner)
Spread into a line. Choose a goal. Then chant,

> *One potato, two potatoes, three potatoes four,*
> *Five potatoes, six potatoes, seven potatoes, MORE.*

After "MORE" the children run as fast as they can to the goal.

CHANT OF THE SEASONS
(A chant-rondo)

Pre-planning

- Composing a chant in rondo form is easy. (See "The Bird Rondo.") Think through the returning part (A) in order to pick up the rhythm of the words. Anticipate what the children might say about each season (parts B, C, D, E).

Musical Focus

- Establishing the concept of rondo form
- Putting thoughts into words to chant

Other Learning

- Introducing the abstract concept of the seasons

Activities and Directions

- *Autumn, winter, spring, and summer, seasons of the year (the A part).*
- Repeat the chant with the children.
- *Today is a day in (autumn).*
- Discuss the current season's weather and holidays. *Is it getting colder or hotter? What color are the leaves? What holidays are coming soon?*
- Lead the children to compose a statement about (autumn) (the B part).
- All recite the statement until it becomes rhythmical.
- Combine the statement with the season chant (A B A). The lesson may end here or after any season.

- Discuss the winter season.
- Develop a statement about winter (the C part).
- Combine the statement with the season chant (A C A).
- Add this to the autumn statement (A B A C A).
- Repeat this routine for spring (A D A), then (A B A C A D A).
- Repeat for summer (A E A), then (A B A C A D A E A).

Continuing Lessons

- Combine the seasons with paper art work for use on a flannel board. A colored leaf may represent autumn; a snowflake, winter; flowers, spring; sunshine, summer. Use the pictures to lead the chant.
- Suggested actions to accompany the chant:
  Seasons—Make a big circle with arms.
  Autumn—Imitate falling leaves with hands.
  Winter—Hug self as if cold.
  Spring—Using the hands to show how flowers grow.
  Summer—Extend arms to show the sun shining or wipe brow as if hot.

  Original actions suggested by the children may better describe their chants.
- Experiment with the autoharp or guitar chords as an accompaniment. Try out drums or bells for sound effects.

THE CLOUDS ARE MAKING PICTURES IN THE SKY

The grass is green and cooling and
   I'm lying on my back;
The clouds are making pictures in the sky.
The clouds are making pictures in the sky.

I see a feather duster and
   It's sweeping up the sky;
A little streak is left across the blue.
The clouds are making pictures in the sky.

I see (Pacific) Ocean waves
   A-rolling upside down;
A school of little fish are swimming by.
The clouds are making pictures in the sky.

I see a map of (Kansas) and
  A picture of a horse;
A puff of dandelion floats away.
The clouds are making pictures in the sky.

I see a lamb and feathered rats,
  And fluffy little chicks;
A polar bear sits on a cloud to think.
The clouds are making pictures in the sky.

Sometimes it's like I'm floating
  And the clouds are standing still;
I'm sailing in a boat made out of grass.
The clouds are making pictures in the sky.

Materials

- Chart paper or chalkboard

Pre-planning

- Read the poem several times to pick up the rhythm.
- Choose verses to which the children can relate.

Musical Focus

- Experiencing the rhythm of descriptive phrases in poetry
- Beginning choric reading

Other Learning

- Poetry as a means of expressing thoughts

Activities and Directions

- *When you watch the clouds you can imagine you see pictures.*
- *This poem is called "The Clouds Are Making Pictures in the Sky."* (Say it lightly with inflection.)
- Have the children repeat this line.
- *In the poem this line is repeated after each verse. Say it with me each time.*
- Read all the poem or the verses previously selected. Encourage the children to join in on the response. Use your hand to help them raise or lower their voices.

- Encourage the children to talk about their cloud pictures. Record their suggestions on chart paper or chalkboard.
- Read a verse selected by the children.
- *When you read poetry your voices make rhythm.*

Continuing Lesson

- Use as an outdoor activity for a day with blue skies and white clouds. (The children may lie on the floor and look out the window.) This is an informal rhythmic and verbalization activity. Do not expect it to be repeated because cloud formations and imagined pictures are always different.

Musical Focus

- Arm and leg rhythm directed toward outlining cloud pictures (arcs, circles, angles, lines and loops)

Other Learning

- Basic information about clouds (moisture, wind, etc.)
- As the children lie on the grass and look up, read the first verse of the poem.
- Suggest that they outline the pictures with their hands or feet and tell about what they imagine.
- Create verses about what the children see.

THE BUG STORY
(A chant and song story)

To Begin

- Establish the beginning pitch; remember it.
- Establish the beat by silently tapping your foot. Keep your foot tapping throughout the story, fitting the speaking, pausing, chanting and singing into the beat. Don't hurry the story.

Teacher: All the boys and girls were looking for bugs.
So I sang: (verse 1)
> "Bug, bug, bug; Do you see that bug? (Point to an imaginary bug.)
> A bug-gy, bug-gy, bug-gy, bug-gy bug, bug, bug."

Children: Repeat.
Teacher: One little boy said: (chant)
> "I see a *bug*, a *big* bug, a *black* bug, a *big* black bug."

Children: Repeat.
Teacher: So I sang: (verse 2)
> "What you see is a beetle bug;
> A beetle, beetle, beetle, beetle, beetle bug."

Children: Repeat.
Teacher: Then one little girl said:
> "I see a *bug*, an *orange* bug, a *spotted* bug, an orange, spotted *bug*."

Children: Repeat.
Teacher: So I sang: (verse 3)
> "What you see is a lady bug;
> A lady, lady, lady, lady, lady bug."

Children: Repeat.
Teacher: And all the boys and girls said:
> "We like *bugs*, *big* bugs, *little* bugs, *big* and little bugs."

Children: Repeat:
Teacher: So I sang: (verse 4)
> "What you like is a big-little bug;
> A big-little, big-little, big-little bug."

Children: Repeat.
Teacher: Then, all the boys and girls laughed and sang: (verse 5)
> "Whoever heard of a big-little bug;
> A big-little, big-little, big-little bug?

Children: Repeat.
All: And that's the bug story.

HEAR THE MOSQUITO

Musical Focus

- Descriptive music and acting out

Activities and Directions

- *Whenever a mosquito is close its humming sounds loud.*
- Sing and act out the song.
- Children sing along and act out.
- Check the ability to hum (in front of closed mouth).
- Have all sing the song again.
- *Mosquitos are a nuisance.*

Songs

THE CLOWN IS SAD

Dm

The clown is sad, he needs to laugh.

(A7)   D

We'll cheer him up, just hear us laugh.

Musical Focus

- Singing in the minor mode
- Creating new sounds or motions to fit the song

Activities and Directions

- *The clown in this song makes other people laugh but he is sad.*
- Sing the song for the children. End by laughing.
- Have the children sing the song, then laugh.
- *What are other things we could do to make the clown laugh?* (Hear us clap, snap, whistle; see us jump, fall, dance.)
- Repeat the song together using new endings.
- *We sang about making the clown laugh.*

Continuing Lessons

- One child may play the D bell, another, the F bell, or one child may play both bells on "The Clown." This may be repeated throughout the song as an ostinato. The words "the clown" may be whispered as the bells are played. This keeps the rhythm steady.

STARS SHINING

Materials

- G and high and low C mallet bells

American Folk Song

Bye'm bye, bye'm bye. Stars shin-ing Shin-ing num-ber one, num-ber 2, num-ber 3, num-ber 4, num-ber 5. Oh my! Bye'm bye, bye'm bye, Oh my Bye'm bye.

Musical Focus

- High and low tones
- Contrast between relaxed and accented singing

Other Learning

- Practice in counting
- Elementary information about stars

Activities and Directions

- *This song is a sleepy song for evening or rest time. When it begins to get dark the stars appear one at a time until the sky is filled with stars.*
- Sing the song.
- Lead a discussion about stars (appearance, distance, etc.).
- All sing the song.
- *Let's sing the counting part of the song. All sing.*
- *Let's sing all the song.*
- Demonstrate how to play the mallet bells.
- *How many stars shall we count this time (up to ten)?*
- Have one child play the G bell, counting the stars as the children sing.
- Sing "Oh, my." Indicate high and low with hand motions.
- Play "Oh, my" on the high and low C bells.
- All sing with full accompaniment.
- *In this song part of the melody goes down and up and part stays close to the same tone.*

Continuing Lessons

- Explore other phrases of the song with mallet bells.
- Count stars with other instruments such as triangle, finger cymbals, or keyboard in a high register.
- Use this song to introduce rest time.
- Relate the song to a number chart.
- Relate to "The First Star Is Lucky."

LOOK AWAY

Materials

- Place available musical instruments in sight, but as far away as possible.

Musical Focus

- Individual singing (responses)

Other Learning

- Recognition of and verbalization about objects in the room

Activities and Directions

- *Sometimes we use field glasses to help us see far away.*
- *We can pretend we have glasses by putting our fists in front of our eyes and looking through the tiny holes.*
- Lead a discussion and experimentation.
- *The first part of the song is for us all.* Sing the first phrase. Have the children repeat it.
- *Then the "Looker" sings about what he/she sees through the holes.* Sing the second phrase. Have the children repeat.

- *We all sing the last part of the song.* Sing it to the children. Then have them repeat it.
- Call on someone to be the "Looker."
- Sing the entire song with the children. Allow the "Looker" complete freedom in the response.
- Mention the instruments but do not name them. Suggest that the "Looker" sing about an instrument.
- Continue with other "Lookers" as time permits.
- Point out each instrument giving the correct name if necessary.
- *You made up little songs about what you saw.*

TRAFFIC LIGHTS

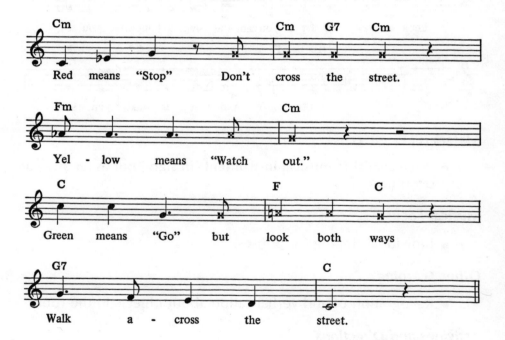

Materials

- Three paper discs (red, yellow, green)

Musical Focus

- Rhythmic dramatization
- Walking tempo

Other Learning

- Safety rules for crossing the street

Activities and Directions

- *It is easier to cross the street when you know what the lights mean.*
- *This song is about crossing the street with traffic lights.*
- Sing the song and illustrate it with the paper discs.
- Discuss the lights and crossing the streets near school.
- All sing the song. Three children hold the discs, raising them when the color is mentioned, lowering them when the next color is mentioned.
- The children dramatize the song. (Disc holders plus two or three children to cross the street)
- *The red, yellow and green discs helped us learn the song and taught us what the traffic lights mean.*
- A verse for crossing without traffic lights:

> **At the curb I stop and wait,**
> **Then I look across.**
> **Next, I look first right, then left;**
> **Then I cross the street.**

THE LARGEST OF THEM ALL

Materials

- (Optional) Pictures of a worm, a bird and a cat

Pre-planning

- A rising melody has a natural feeling of increasing volume. Notice the gradations in singing (whisper-singing, soft singing, normal singing, and loud singing).

Musical Focus

- Crescendo on a rising melody (C major triad)

Other Learning

- Developing concepts of comparative sizes

Activities and Directions

- *Some creatures are very small and some are larger.*

- *A worm is very small; a bird is larger than a worm; a cat is larger than a bird; a child is the largest of them all.*
- Discuss sizes (Use pictures.) and experiences of the children.
- Whisper-sing on low C:
  I am a worm, a wiggly, wiggly worm. Have the children repeat it.
- Sing softly on E:
  I am a bird; I sit in a tree. Have the children repeat it.
  Sing in a normal singing voice on G:
  I am a cat. "Meow, meow, meow." Have the children repeat it.
- Sing in a loud voice on high C:
  I am a child, the largest of them all. Have the children repeat it.
- *Your singing began softly with the small worm and became louder and louder.*

Continuing Lessons

- Singing about and describing with movement may also help to bridge the gap between concepts of the tangible and the intangible. An improvised map will be helpful.
  This is our school.
  This is our town.
  This is our state.
  This is our country.
- A verse for creative action:
  I am a grasshopper; a-light, a-light, a-light.
  I am a rabbit; a-hop, a-hop, a-hop.
  I am a fox; a-sneak, a-sneak, a-sneak.
  I am (name), the largest of them all.
- Reverse the lines, singing the highest and loudest first, and gradually decreasing the volume (descrescendo).

HIGH IN SKY
(Two Lessons)

Materials

- Keyboard or other instrument ($\underline{C}$,E, G,$\overline{C}$)

Pre-planning

- Play lines one and two together on a keyboard or bells to hear the intervals (Fifths $\underline{C}$ - G, and sixths E - $\overline{C}$).

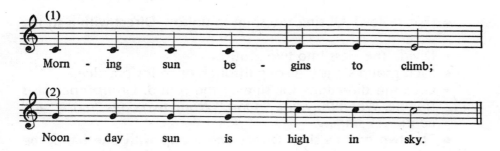

Morn - ing sun be - gins to climb;

Noon - day sun is high in sky.

Musical Focus

- Developing independent singing on pitch
- First experience in singing in harmony

Other Learning

- Cooperation of two groups to produce music together

Activities and Directions

Lesson 1

- *The melody in this song moves up like the sun in the morning.*
- Sing the song indicating the direction of the melody with your hand(s).
- The children sing the song with you, also using their hand(s).
- Repeat the song, exaggerating the accents. Have the children repeat it at least twice.
- Play the line not being sung by the children as an accompaniment.
- Discuss the resulting harmony.
- *When two tones are sounded together there is harmony.*
- To determine the readiness of the children for singing in harmony (singing the song as a round) use this procedure:
  1. All sing the song with "loo" or hum it. (Check pitch.)
  2. One half of the children sing line 1 while the other children sing line 2. Reverse the groups. Encourage careful listening by the children.

Lesson 2

- *This song is a round. We will all sing the song but we will start at two different times.*

- (For review) All sing the song in unison. Direct with a strong accent.
- Divide the class into two groups.
- Each group sings the song through once for practice.
- Give the directions for singing the round. *Group one starts singing. When they sing "noon," group two sings "morn" and continues singing.*
- The two groups sing. Direct one group with one hand, the other group with the other hand.
- Discuss the harmony produced.
- Repeat the round, this time singing it through two times.
- If the group is ready, reverse the groups and sing again.
- *We can sing a round many times with one group following the other group around and around.*

Continuing Lessons

- Use the C, E, G, and C̄ bells to play the melody and later to accompany the round.

JAPANESE RAIN SONG

1. Pit - ter pat - ter, fall - ing, fall - ing, Rain is fall - ing down.
2. Un - der-neath the droop - ing wil - low, Stands a lit - tle child;
3. A - me, a - me fu - re, fu - re, Ka - a - san - ga,

Moth - er comes to bring um - brel - la, Rain is fall - ing down.
No um - brel - la, child is weep - ing, Rain is fall - ing down.
Ja - no me de o mu - kae, U - re - shi - na.

Pi - chi Pi - chi cha - pu cha - pu ran ran ran.
(pronounced) pee - chee cha - pu Ran

"Japanese Rain Song" from Sing a Song of People *by Roberta McLaughlin and Lucille Wood. Copyright 1973 by Bowmar/Noble Publishers, Inc. Used by permission of publisher.*

Materials

- Several sets of chopsticks, pencils, rhythm sticks, or twigs

Pre-planning

- Experiment with stick sounds

Musical Focus

- Uneven rhythm (imitating rain)
- Singing lightly

Activities and Directions

- *What are some of the sounds that the rain makes as it falls?*
- The children respond with their rain sounds. (Pitter-patter, drip-drop, etc.)
- Sing the first verse.
- *Pichi, etc.* are rain sounds in this Japanese song.
- The children repeat after you the last phrase—one measure at a time.
- All sing the complete song.
- Hand out the sticks. Let the children experiment with holding and tapping. (Holding near one end and tapping near the other end make the best sounds.)
- Sing the song as the children make the rain sounds. Emphasize the long-short rhythm.
- Combine the children's suggested sounds and the stick sounds for an introduction to the song.
- Sing the song with introduction and stick accompaniment.
- *Your stick sounds and singing are like rain music.*

Continuing Lessons

- Accompany the song by plucking the G on autoharp or other stringed instrument. (C - G or C - G - A - G are more elaborate accompaniments.)
- Relate the song to a discussion of the proper use of an umbrella.

LET IT GROW

Focus

- Call and response (pre-ballad singing)

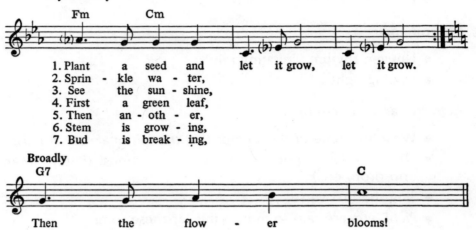

- Singing in the minor mode, then changing to major
- Finger clapping to keep the beat

Other Learning

- Awareness of plant growth pattern
- Learning to sequence events

Activities and Directions

- *This song tells how a seed grows into a flower.*
- *Listen to part of the song, "Let it grow, let it grow."*
- Have the children repeat the phrase.
- *Sing and finger clap it with me.* Children repeat.
- Sing "Plant a seed and." Invite the response.
- Continue the verses and responses.
- End the song with the major phrase, "Then the flower blooms." Have the children repeat it.
- *Sing it all with me this time.* Children sing call and response.
- *This song has many verses but one part is always the same.*

Continuing Lessons

- Lead the children in creating a dramatic dance.
- Plant radish seeds or beans in paper cups. Make up verses to record the growth of the plants.
- Relate the song to an art lesson.
- Halloween activity to sing and act out.
  - (1) Spooks appear on Halloween, Halloween.
  - (2) Watch for ghosts on Halloween, Halloween.
  - (3) Jack-o-lanterns, Halloween, Halloween.
  - (4) Witches scream on Halloween, Halloween.

  Ending: This is Halloween.

IT SINGS UP TO THE SKY
(Two Lessons)

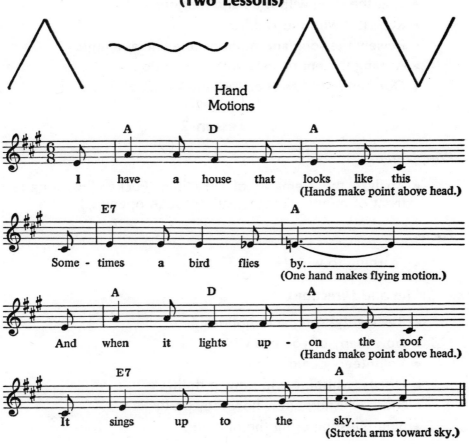

Hand Motions

I have a house that looks like this
(Hands make point above head.)

Some-times a bird flies by.
(One hand makes flying motion.)

And when it lights up-on the roof
(Hands make point above head.)

It sings up to the sky.
(Stretch arms toward sky.)

Lesson 1

Pre-planning

- Prepare to lead the suggested hand motions (or plan others).

Musical Focus

- Dramatizing a song with the hands and arms

Other Learning

- Coordination of hands, images, words

Activities and Directions

- *We can all sing.*
- Sing the song with the hand motions.
- Repeat it with the children.
- Review the song and motions one line at a time.
- All sing the entire song with the motions.
- *Our hands and arms act out the words of the song.*

Lesson 2

Pre-planning

- Analyze the elements of whistling. (Pucker lips, tongue to front of mouth. Force breath through opening.)

Focus

- Learning to whistle

Activities and Directions

- Review the song and motions.
- *How many of you can whistle?*
- Volunteers demonstrate.
- Discuss whistling and how to do it.
- More whistlers show how they do it.
- Sing the song using the motions.

- Whistle the song and do the motions.
- *When children whistle they sound like birds singing.*

Continuing Lessons

- Use other verses with new actions.

**I have a yard that looks like this. (Stretch arms
out.)
Sometimes my cat comes by. (Hand indicates cat.)
She softly sits upon the grass (One hand strokes
the other.)
And purrs and says, "Meow."
(Repeat, singing "Meow.")**

**I have a porch that looks like this. (Make a big
square.)
Sometimes my dog comes by. (Indicate dog.)
He wags his tail and sits by me (Pat dog on the
head.)
And barks and says, "Bow wow."**

(Repeat singing "Bow, wow, wow, wow.")

SKIP TO MY LOU

Lou, Lou, Skip to my Lou; Lou, Lou, Skip to my Lou.

Lou, Lou, Skip to my Lou; Skip to my Lou, my dar - ling.

Pre-planning

- Review individual verbalization abilities and needs.

Musical Focus

- Vigorous rhythm (Review skipping progress.)
- Adding nonsensical verses (humor in music)

Other Learning

- Vocabulary building (introduction to antonyms and reasons for humor)

Activities and Directions

- *Listen to this skipping song.* Sing the song.
- Sing the song with the children.
- All sing again, clapping.
- Volunteers skip to the singing and clapping.
- *This is a funny verse:*

  Sing, *"Little red wagon, painted blue (three times),
    Skip to my Lou, my darling."*
- Discuss the words. Why is it impossible? funny?
- All sing the song.
- *What other funny things could we sing about?*
  (I'm standing up while I'm sitting down.)
  (I'm very hot and I'm very cold.)
- *Let's sing all our funny verses.*

Continuing Lessons

- Add autoharp and/or percussion instruments to the song.
- Make up other nonsense verses like:

  "My little dog, he thinks he's a cat."
  "Round and round and upside down."

- (An easy circle game) *Balladeer*
  1. The children skip around the circle singing the first verse. The *Balladeer* stands in the middle.
  2. The *Balladeer* sings a verse while the children stand still and clap.
  3. The children circle and sing the *Balladeer's* verse while the *Balladeer* chooses the next *Balladeer,* then takes his/her place in the circle.
  4. Repeat any number of times.

Rhythmic Body Language

GOLDFISH

Materials

- Mallet bells and/or keyboard
- (Optional) goldfish

Pre-planning

- Become familiar with the mallet bells and keyboard. (Hold the mallet near the end; strike center of the bar. For glissando, draw the mallet across all the bars leading with the wrist. On the keyboard make a glissando by drawing the back of a fingernail across the keys, leading with the wrist.)

Musical Focus

- Speaking with inflection leading to improvisational singing
- Descriptive words guiding rhythmic movements of the whole body and limbs; feeling musical sounds going up and down

Other Learning

- Perception of water movements, goldfish

Activities and Directions

- Repeat the lyrics with the children until they develop a definite pulse.
- Pick up the pulse with light but steady finger or toe tapping.
- Continue the lyrics emphasizing the words, "up, down, around."

> Goldfish live in water;
> They swim around and up;
> Then down, around and up again;
> They swim around and up.

- Play glissandos on "up" and "down."
- Volunteers play glissandos.
- All repeat the lyrics with glissando accompaniment.
- Invite the children to "sing" the lyrics. Emphasize inflection.
- The children "swim" as they sing. Volunteers continue to play the glissando background.
- *Melody can go up or down or stay the same.*

Continuing Lessons

- The children may improvise verses about feeding the fish, antics of the fish.
- Relate the "Goldfish" to the lesson on "The Aquarium."

MAKE AN A, B, C

Materials

- Arm's length floor space for each child
- Letter chart

Musical Focus

- Creating letters using limbs, heads and torso
- Putting body shaped letters into a rhythmical framework
- Beginning concept of formal organization in music

Other Learning

- Increasing body awareness
- Reinforcing visual concept of upper-case letters

Activities and Directions

Part 1. Creating the Letters

- *If you move yourself just right, you can make letter shapes.*
- *How can we make an A?* (Stand straight, legs apart, one arm close to side, other arm bent at elbow across waist)
- Have the children experiment; refer to letter chart.
- After discussion and agreement, all make an A.
- *How can we make a B?* (Stand straight with left arm close to

side, right arm bent with hand on hip; right knee bent to the right and toe pointed on floor.)
- Have the children experiment; refer to letter chart; practice.
- All make a B.
- *How can we make a C?* (Bend waist to the right; bend upper body toward the left, arms together above head).
- Let the children experiment; refer to chart; practice.
- All make a C.
- *Let's all make an A (pause), B (pause), C (pause).*

Part 2. Putting the Letters into Rhythms

- *This is one way to make letters into a rhythm.*
- Chant slowly and clap to keep the beat, as positions are assumed, held, then relaxed.
- *Make an A.* (hold, relax)
- *Make a B.* (hold, relax)
- *Make a C.* (hold, relax)
- *This is an A, B, C Dance.* (teacher directed)
- Divide the class into three groups of eight. (If there are more than 24, use partners.) Group 1 is A; group 2 is B; group 3 is C.
- Sing the letters as you point and direct the individuals in each group to assume the letter position (and hold) in quick succession.

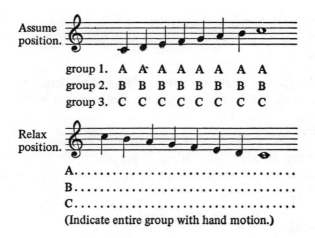

Continuing Lessons

- Children explore ways to create their initials. Then the teacher and children chant, *(A) is for (Alfred). Watch (Alfred) spell.* Move quickly to give all the children an opportunity to participate.
- The children create their own letter dance.

LISTEN, LISTEN TO THE CLOCK

Lis - ten, lis - ten to the clock, "Tick - a, tick - a, tick - a tock,"

On the wall or on the shelf, "Tick - a, tick - a," by it - self.

Tick - a, tick - a, tick - a tock, Tick - a, tick - a tock.

Materials

- (Optional) A clock that ticks

Pre-planning

- Gauge approximate duration of a second. Experiment with finger tapping. Practice, watching the second hand.

Musical Focus

- Listening to and recreating even rhythmic sounds with small movements (snapping fingers, clapping knees together, moving toes)

Other Learning

- Developing body awareness and potentials

Activities and Directions

Part 1
- *Lie on your back with your feet on the floor and your knees high.*
- (Optional) Have the children listen to the clock tick.
- *Listen to me as I snap my fingers, then join me.*
- *Keep snapping your fingers while you slap your knees together. Keep a steady beat.* (The tendency will be to speed up.)
- *Keep snapping and slapping and start moving your toes in rhythm (not the heels). You are doing three things at once. You are like little clocks with parts moving.* (Stop motions.)

Part 2
- *How many parts did you move at one time?* Discuss this.
- *Can you think of other ways to keep time?* (Clicking tongue)
- *As I sing the new clock song, help me keep time with your fingers, knees, and toes and any other way you can.*
- Sing the song with the children's movements as an accompaniment.
- *Your moving kept time for the new song.*
- Have everyone sing the song once with or without accompaniment.

Continuing Lessons

- Review the song. Use wood block, sticks, pencil on table or other soft sharp sound for an accompaniment.
- Add bells or keyboard to measures 1, 2 and 5 ($\overline{C}$, G, A, G).
- Use the song for part of a mat exercise lesson.
- Relate it to a walk around the building to see the clocks, or a trip to a clock store.

Basic Rhythms

WATCH ME

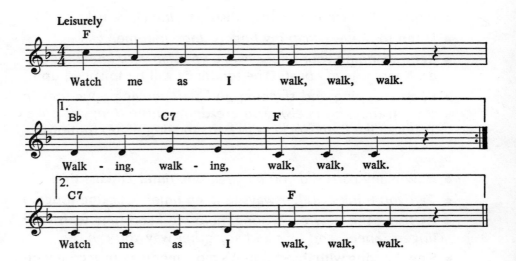

Leisurely

Watch me as I walk, walk, walk.

1. Walk - ing, walk - ing, walk, walk, walk.

2. Watch me as I walk, walk, walk.

Materials

- Hand drum (You may substitute slapping or striking wood.)
- Floor space for walking

Pre-planning

- Work out drum accompaniments.
  Walk; hop (one foot)
  Run-a
  Jump (two feet)

Musical Focus

- One or more basic foot movements in even rhythm and directed by the words of the song

Other Learning

- Self-evaluation of performance ("I am a good jumper.")

Activities and Directions

- *Can your feet keep time to this even beat?*
- Play the drum beat for walking while children keep time with their feet. (If seated, have heels on the floor, toes tapping.)
- Sing the song keeping time on the drum.
- Children repeat the song with teacher's help.
- Volunteers walk while others sing and tap feet.
- If floor space permits, everyone may walk.
- Volunteer may play the drum.
- *Can your feet do something else to this music?* (Hop)
- Volunteers demonstrate, or all hop.
- *We can use the same music for walking and hopping.*

Continuing Lessons

- Focus on walking and running.
- Focus on walking and jumping.
- Review all one-step rhythms.

WE JUMP AND WALK, WALK, WALK

We jump   and walk, walk, walk.   We jump   and walk, walk, walk.

Materials

- Floor space for a small group

Musical Focus

- Contrast of slow and fast demonstrated by rhythms (two actions)

Other Learning

- Transition from a single action to a combination of actions

Activities and Directions

- *Feet jump together. (Demonstrate.)*
- *Feet walk one at a time.*
- *Let's practice our walking. (Repeat: Walk, walk, walk.)*
- *Follow the directions of the words as we all sing.*
- Repeat the song two or three times.
- *What kind of animal jumps? (kangaroo) Show me.*
- *What kind of animal walks? (horse, dog, elephant, etc.) Show me.*
- *Sing and jump like a (kangaroo) and walk like a (horse).*

Continuing Lesson

- Relate the song and rhythms to a lesson about the zoo.
- Combine the one-step rhythms ("Watch Me") with this lesson. Create a dance.

GALLOPING

Materials

- Floor space for gallopers
- Wood block, coconut cymbals or rhythm sticks
- (Optional) Picture of a horse galloping

Pre-planning

- Developmentally, galloping precedes skipping. It is a high walking step followed by a running step-together with the rear foot. The same foot continues to lead.

Musical Focus

- Learning to gallop to music (physically feeling the uneven rhythm)

Other Learning

- Consciously coordinating foot patterns

Activities and Directions

- *We are going to gallop like horses.*
- Discuss horses (and show pictures) and any experiences children may have had with horses.
- Ask for volunteers to gallop without accompaniment. Pick up the rhythm (♩   ♪) from the galloper and establish it by slapping thighs (patsching), then singing the song. If no child can gallop, demonstrate, with one child on each side of you.
- Have all sing and patsch.
- Volunteers get ready to gallop (introduction), then gallop, singing or not as they please. (The teacher and other children sing.) Add (wood block) to emphasize the rhythm.
- To stop the galloping, accent the word "Whoa" as a directive.
- *This class of good gallopers is ready for a rest.*

A SKIPPING SONG
(The Farmer in the Dell)

Materials

- Floor space or playground

Pre-planning

- Analyze the skipping procedure (step-hop on one foot then on the other).

Skip, a-skip, a - skip,___ a - skip, a-skip, a - skip.___

Hap - py day, a hap - py day, a - skip, a-skip, a - skip.___

Musical Focus

- Learning to skip to music
- Establishing the feeling for uneven rhythm (long-short)

Activities and Directions

- *First we skip on one foot then on the other.*
- *Does anyone know how to skip?* (If there is a volunteer, note the child's skipping tempo as a guide for the tempo of the song.)
- Sing the skipping song.
- Invite a child to skip with you. (Hold hands.)
- Have volunteers try skipping. (Some may revert to galloping.) Skip with anyone still unsure or have a child who knows how to skip help the other children.
- *You are good skippers. You will have lots of room to skip outdoors.*

Continuing Lessons

- Review the entire lesson.
- Add instrumental accompaniment (drum, autoharp, etc.).
- Allow free skipping. (Plan a traffic route to avoid collisions.)
- Play the game "The Farmer in the Dell."

  Verses: "The farmer in the dell, the farmer in the dell, Heigh-o, the derry-o, the farmer in the dell."
  Verses 2, 3, 4, 5, 6, 7, 8: "The farmer takes a wife (child, nurse, dog, cat, rat, cheese)."
  Verse 9: "The cheese stands alone."

● To play: Children form a circle with "farmer" inside. As they join hands, circle and sing, the farmer chooses a "wife" to join him in the circle. On the cheese verse children stand still and clap. Cheese becomes the next farmer.

OATS, PEAS, BEANS AND BARLEY GROW
(two-part lesson)
(An Introduction to Formal Singing Games)

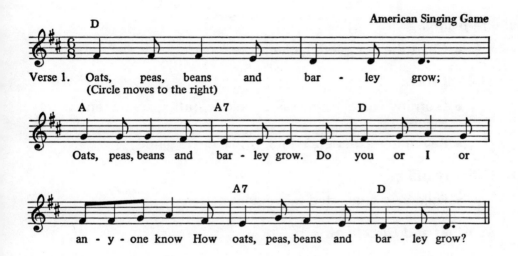

Verse 1. Oats, peas, beans and bar-ley grow;
(Circle moves to the right)

Oats, peas, beans and bar-ley grow. Do you or I or

an-y-one know How oats, peas, beans and bar-ley grow?

Verse 2. (All stand. Farmer leads actions.)

First the farmer sows his seed (sweeping arm motion),
Then he stands and takes his heed (hands on hips),
He stamps his foot and claps his hands,
And turns around to view the land.

Verse 3. (Circle moves to the *left*.)

Waiting for a partner,
Waiting for a partner,
Break the ring and take one in
While we dance and while we sing. (Farmer brings a partner into the circle.)

Verse 4. (Circle continues to the *left*. Farmer and partner skip to *right*.)

Tra, la la la la la la etc.

(At the end of verse, farmer joins the circle and his/her partner becomes the new farmer.)

Materials

- (Optional) Pictures of crops growing
- Floor space for circle

Pre-planning

- Chart the complete game route.

Musical Focus

- Learning verses to the same melody; fitting actions and words together
- Beginning experience in a formal circle game

Other Learning

- Following a directed movement pattern

Activities and Directions

Part 1

- *This is a singing game about a farmer who grows things to eat.*
- Sing the first verse.
- Discuss the meaning of the words (and show pictures).
- *Sometimes we eat oats in oatmeal cookies or cereal; peas with carrots; beans in chili; and barley in soup.*
- Explain the game action for verse 1. (Indicate "you or I.")
- All sing, swaying to the *right*.
- Introduce verse 2 and actions.
- Have all of the children sing, swaying to the *left*.
- Repeat the entire song. Demonstrate the entire game with a small group of children. This may be repeated with several small groups.
- *Now we are ready to play the singing game.*

Part 2 (Challenging)

- *"In verse 1 the circle skips to the right. In verse 2 we all stand still and watch the farmer. In verse 3 the circle skips to the left while the farmer chooses a partner. They skip inside the circle as we all keep moving and singing "Tra la."*
- Review the song and actions, walking through the game.
- Form a circle. (Join hands and lead the children into a circle, or draw a chalk circle and let children form the circle by putting their toes on the chalk line.)
- All sing as the leader directs the game through once slowly.
- Play the game again at normal skipping tempo.
- Repeat the game as time and interest permit.

THE FINGERS

The fin - gers · on my right hand are like the ones on left
(Hold up right hand, fingers spread. Keep time.   Hold up left hand.)

I touch them all, See how they fit; 1 2 3 4 5 all.____
(Touch matching fingers   Touch corresponding fingers. Clap.)

Musical Focus

- Moving left and right hands, and fingers, to music
- Reviewing uneven (long-short) rhythm

Activities and Directions

- *Spread out the fingers on your right hand, and your left.*
- Sing the first line. Demonstrate the actions, turning away from the children so your right hand is on their right. Check right and left hands.
- Sing the second line slowly with actions.
- Have everyone sing and try the hand actions.
- Have the children sing the whole song. Emphasize the long-short rhythm.
- *Let's sing the song and act it out as fast as we can.*

Continuing Lesson

- Sing these verses for another finger play.

> **My thumb is like a monster and moves all by itself.**
> **My pointer finger points and bends and makes a little shelf.**
>
> **My middle finger — longest one; the next one's for my ring.**
> **My little one can touch my thumb. And that's all I will sing.**

TIP TODDLE
(Three-tone song)

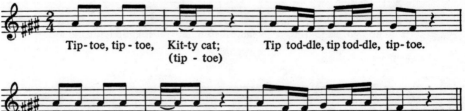

Tip-toe, tip-toe, Kit-ty cat;   Tip tod-dle, tip tod-dle, tip-toe.
(tip - toe)

Tip-toe, tip-toe, Kit-ty cat;   Tip tod-dle, tip tod-dle, toe.
(tip - toe)

Special Preparation

- (Optional) Children take off shoes

Musical Focus

- Toe rhythms
- Nonsense syllables to music

Other Learning

- Awareness of toe movements
- Potentials of mouth sounds

Activities and Directions

- *Your toes can keep the beat for this kitty-cat song.*
- Sing the song. The children keep time with their toes.
- Review the song one phrase at a time. If necessary slow down and chant the words.
- Have all sing the song two or three times, keeping time with their toes.
- Let the children explore the possibilities of toe movements. Discuss this.
- Have all sing the song once more, moving toes in rhythm.
- *Our toes keep the beat like little kitty-cat paws.*

Continuing Lessons

- Sing the song with tiptoe rhythms (walking like kittens).
- Add an instrumental accompaniment. One child may keep time on the A# bell or keyboard for phrases 1 and 3 and on A# and F# for phrases 2 and 4.

Imitative and Free Rhythms

RIDING MY BICYCLE UPSIDE DOWN

1. Rid - ing my bi - cy - cle____ up - side down;
Repeat: whistle
2. Where can I go when I'm____ up - side down,____ I'll
Repeat: whistle

wheels turn - ing 'round and 'round, I'm up - side down.

bi - cy - cle to the sky, I'm up - side down.

Materials

- Mats or ample floor space or lawn for each child (lying down)

Pre-planning

- Floor or mat rhythms encourage relaxation with no fear of falling. They also provide exercises different from upright rhythms. Anticipate balance between movement and relaxation.

Musical Focus

- Using limbs in rhythms
- Reinforcing the concept of fast and slow
- Practicing whistling

Other Learning

- Awareness of "above" and what is there
- Exploration of the upside down perspective

Activities and Directions

- *Lie on your back and look up.*
- *Rest before you start your upside down bicycle ride. (Can you really ride a bicycle upside down?)*
- *Let me see you pedal your bicycle upside down.*
- Sing the first verse as they pedal.
- Have the children lie still as they repeat the song.
- All sing and pedal.
- Have all rest and whistle the melody.
- Briefly discuss what hands and feet do on a bicycle.
- Sing the second verse.
- Have everyone sing the second verse and ride the imaginary upside down bicycle.
- *Ride your bicycle as fast as you can as we sing both verses. (Gradually slow to a stop.)*
- *Your feet made your bicycles move in time with the music.*

Continuing Lessons

- Review or relearn the song. Focus on the second verse and what you can see when you look up. Relate to "The Clouds Are Making Pictures in the Sky."
- Floor activities developing concepts of under, over, through, and between:

Crawling and crawling under the bridge;
Crawling, I'm crawling under the bridge.(cardboard resting on two chairs)

"over the hill" (stacked mats, pillows, small barrel)
"*through* the tunnel" (barrel, cloth draped over two chairs)
"between the trees (between the two tallest things in the room or two chairs)

- Wake up verse:

Animals in cages cannot run;
Stretching and turning is their fun.

ONE ELEPHANT

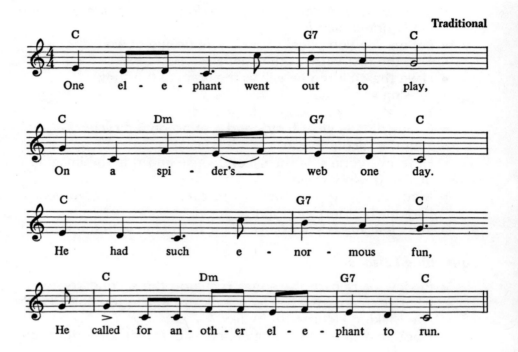

Traditional

One el - e - phant went out to play,
On a spi - der's___ web one day.
He had such e - nor - mous fun,
He called for an - oth - er el - e - phant to run.

Materials

- Low drum
- (Optional) Picture of an elephant

Pre-planning

- Anticipate: (1) the ways children might imitate an elephant walking, (2) the tempo of walk tapped on a drum.

Musical Focus

- Slow, even rhythm
- Humorous dramatic play in music

Other Learning

- How large animals move
- Building vocabulary (ridiculous)

Activities and Directions

- *Listen to this ridiculous happening.*
- *Isn't "ridiculous" a good word?* Discuss its meaning and repeat it several times together.
- Sing the first two lines of the song. (*Could an elephant really play on a spider's web? That's ridiculous.*)
- All sing. Accompany the singing with a soft drum beat.
- Discuss the situation. How does an elephant walk? How does its trunk move?
- A volunteer demonstrates as all sing.
- Add the last two lines.
- Have a volunteer choose another elephant. *How can the new elephant hold onto elephant number one?* (trunk grasps tail—hand grasps hand)
- Repeat the song with "two elephants, etc." The second elephant chooses a third. The third chooses a fourth.
- *These elephants are moving slowly and carefully to the music.*
- **The lesson may end here or continue.**
- Sing the last verse, *All elephants went out to play (etc.)*, ending, *They broke the web 'cause they weighed a ton.*
- For an orderly return to seats, teacher may lead a parade line with each trunk holding tail (hand) of elephant in front. Children drop out of the parade when they reach their seats.

Continuing Lessons

- Choreograph the action for a formal program.
- Make up other ridiculous verses as an exercise in verbal expression, e.g., *One little rabbit hopped out to play, In a big apple tree one day.*
- On the playground or sidewalk (solo play) *tried to miss the cracks in the sidewalk way.*

I AM SKATING
(Two Parts)

Materials

- Ample floor space for all (If space is limited, small groups may take turns.)

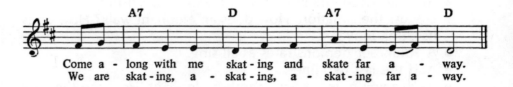

Pre-planning

- Review the skating step. (a long, sliding step with the right foot, arms swinging to the right; a long, sliding step with the left foot, arms swinging to the left).

Musical Focus

- Experiencing triple rhythm with a skating step and whole body movement

Other Learning

- (Part 2) Beginning concept of moving in couples

Activities and Directions

Part 1

- *In the summer we roller skate. In the winter we ice skate.*
- Discussion *(Did you ever go skating? How do you learn to skate? Why do you like to skate?)*
- *How do you move when you are skating?* Discuss this.
- *This is a skating song.* Sing the first verse, swaying from side to side to emphasize the rhythm.
- All repeat the verse and swaying.
- Have all of the children do the skating step as they sing. Demonstrate the step with your back to the children so they may copy the step exactly.
- *You skate to one side, then to the other side with the rhythm.*

Part 2 (Challenging)

- Sing the song again. This time do the skating step and add verse two. Take the hand of the child nearest you and do the skating step together as you sing.
- Break with this child. Each of you takes a new partner.
- This continues until all the children are singing and skating.
- *When you skate with someone else your feet move in the same direction.*

Continuing Lessons

- Incorporate the song and rhythm into a winter program.
- Partners "skate" holding hands in the traditional cross arm position.

A GIANT MAN DANCES

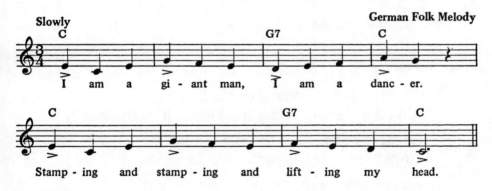

Materials

- Floor space for 8 stamps forward
- Chording instrument and/or drum

Musical Focus

- Establishing the feeling of triple rhythm and strong accents

Activities and Directions

- *A giant man has big heavy feet but he can dance.*
- *How would a giant man dance?* (heavy stamp) (Volunteers demonstrate.)

- *This song is a giant man's dance. As I sing, think how you will dance like a giant man. (Sing with a heavy accent.)*
- *Let's all sing and dance. (Drum or heavy chord accompaniment.)*
- *Turn around and dance back. (Eight stamps back.)*
- *A big heavy step is a stamp. It is a good step for giant dancing.*

BEAUTIES OF HAWAII

Ha - wai - an flow'r, I wear it in___ my hair;

I sway and step and touch the flow'r, I wear it in___ my hair.

Other Verses

A shell of pink, I found it on the beach;
I hold the shell up to my ear; I found it on the beach.

The air is warm, I see the sky of blue;
I stretch my arms up to the sky; I see the sky of blue.

In water clear, I swish and swash my feet;
I ride a wave and splash the foam; I swish and swash
    my feet.

Materials

- Autoharp, guitar, or keyboard
- (Optional) Pictures of Hawaii

Musical Focus

- Coordinating rhythmical movements with words and melody

Other Learning

- Introductory facts about Hawaii

Activities and Directions

- *Across the ocean in warm Hawaii there are beautiful flowers.*
- Sing the first verse, swaying as you sing.
- The children repeat the singing and swaying.
- Discuss Hawaii. (Show pictures.)
- Have everyone sing the first verse again. Accompany this with slow sweeping chords.
- Children repeat the verse and experiment with appropriate actions.
- Choose and sing another verse. Help the children make up appropriate actions.
- Have all sing both verses with actions and accompaniment.
- *In the song you described some of the beauties of Hawaii.*

Continuing Lessons

- Sing other verses and make up actions.
- Accompany the song with the ipu (a large hollow gourd).

  To play the ipu: With one hand hold the ipu by the neck. Slap the side with the other hand. To add variety, tap the ipu lightly on the floor, strike it with a pencil, or put pebbles or small shells inside and shake it.

- Add a formal dance. An effective foot pattern for well coordinated children is—(step) right, together, step, hold; left, together, step, hold. Evaluate the ability of the children before teaching this step.

WE SING, WE MOVE

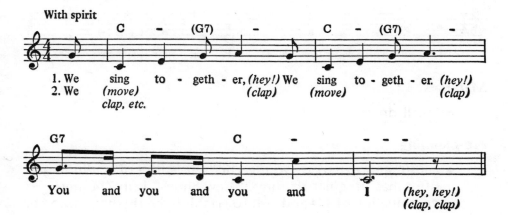

Musical Focus

- Rhythmic movement to a syncopated beat (in this case emphasis on count 4)
- The first verse establishes the melody and rhythm and sets the stage for movement. In each verse a different part of the body moves to the beat.

Other Learning

- Physical exercise (wake up, rainy day, tension breaker)

Activities and Directions

- Sing the song. *Let's sing it together.*
- *How can we move as we sing the song?*
- Sing and move, using the children's suggestions.
- *We kept the rhythm of the song when we moved.*

Suggestions for Movement

- Sitting: snap fingers, clap hands, move wrists, flap arms, wiggle toes, move ankles, lift and lower knees, lift feet, sway from side to side, bend forward or backward, move head, lift shoulders, blink eyes, move facial muscles.
- Standing: stretch, bend from the waist, stamp, jump, hop, walk, run, gallop, skip.

NEW SHOES

Heard in a shopping center

I am wear - ing new shoes; I am wear - ing new shoes.

Materials

- Small drum

Pre-planning

- Music improvised by young children is free of tradition and often has irregular rhythms. "New Shoes" is in 7/4 meter—a combination of 4/4 and 3/4. To establish the rhythmic swing of the song, sing it with 1, 2, 3, 4, 5, 6, 7, stamping on count 1 and lunging forward, arms swinging freely.

Musical Focus

- Feeling and expressing a rhythm with the feet and whole body

Other Learning

- Encouraging pride in clothing

Activities and Directions

- *Sometimes we sing because we are proud of our new clothes.*
- *I think someone has a new pair of shoes today.* (clean, polished, boots, etc.)
- *Show the (new shoes) to us.*
- Sing "(John) is wearing new shoes." Emphasize count one.
- Invite the children to sing with you.
- Continue the singing together adding the stamping and lunging.
- Tap a drum on counts 7 and 1 as an accompaniment.
- *New shoes (or other clothing) are good things to sing about. Let's pretend we all have new shoes and sing the song again.*
- All sing.

Other Verses

"See my zipper jacket."
"I am wearing mittens."
"See my new blue jeans."

Singing, Moving, and Listening

The Note Book of Anna Magdalena Bach
(around 1720)
by Johann Sebastian Bach
and other members of his family

March in D Major (strong accents), Musette in D Major (busy and playful), Minuet in G Major and Minuet in G Minor (both good pieces for feeling triple rhythm) are all from the note book of pieces Bach (a great German musician who lived before George Washington was president) wrote for his wife and many children. Others in the family also contributed to the family's study of music.

Easy to play, short, and cheerful, these pieces are a good source for the teacher who plays the piano. Use them for rhythms, story improvisations, original songs, quiet listening. See "Programs for Children," Part 5.

A LITTLE NIGHT MUSIC
adapted from Romanze from *Eine kleine Nachtmusik*
(Serenade in G, K. 525)
by Wolfgang Amadeus Mozart
(Austria: 1756–1791)

Night is here;— sky is dark and moon is high. Stars twin - kle,

stars twin - kle; It is time for sleep - ing — hum.—

Musical Focus

- Learning a calm and relaxing song
- Learning a theme from a famous composition

72

Activities and Directions

- *After the sun goes down the light is gone and it is night.*
- *Our new song describes the night.*
- Sing the song.
- Talk about the dark sky, the moon, stars, sleep.
- Sing the song again with the children.
- Repeat.
- *When you sang the song you told me about the night.*

Continuing Lesson

Materials

- Recording (Bowmar Orchestral Library—Fashions in Music 101) or Adventures in Music (Record Library for Elementary School—RCA Victor LE 1004)
- (Optional) Pictures of violin, viola, cello, bass

Pre-planning

- This piece is in rondo form (A B A C A coda—a short added conclusion). The instruments are violin, viola, cello, and bass. The "Night Music" song uses the melody of the A or returning part. Listen several times to familiarize yourself with the themes and instrumentation.

Musical Focus

- Recognition of a familiar melody
- The string instruments

Activities and Directions

- *Listen to this melody. Where did you hear it before?* (Play only the A part.) (It will be played an octave above the children's song.)
- Discuss the melody.
- Sing the song (*Night Music*).
- All the instruments have strings. Name the instruments. (Show pictures.)
- When you hear your song, raise your hand.
- Play the recording (all).
- *Did you hear the stringed instruments playing your song?* (three times)

BLUE DANUBE WALTZ
(Opus 314)
by Johann Strauss
(Austria: 1804–1849)

Materials

- Recording
- 24″ ribbons or narrow strips of paper (one for each child)
- Ample floor space for individuals to swing ribbons

Pre-planning

- The entire piece takes about 9½ minutes which is long for uninterrupted, concentrated listening. You may use only a part of the piece, stopping at the end of any section. (The entire piece is excellent as background music for an art or craft lesson.)

Musical Focus

- Moving to a regular waltz rhythm
- Creating a ribbon dance

Activities and Directions

- *How will you move to this music?*
- Play a short section of the piece. Let volunteers demonstrate.
- *Let's swing our arms to the music.* (Make figure eights in the air.)
- Give each child a ribbon.
- Children spread out with ample room in between.
- Play the piece while the children keep time with the ribbons.
- *You did a ribbon dance to the music.*

THE AQUARIUM
from *The Carnival of the Animals*
by C. Saint-Saëns
(France: 1835–1921)

Materials

- Recording (Bomar Orchestra Library 064)

- Floor space—arm's length for each child
- (Optional) An aquarium, fish bowl, or picture of one

Pre-planning

- Become familiar with the music—the mood, changes, length, good places to stop

Musical Focus

- Listening and moving to program (picture) music

Other Learning

- Names, characteristics, and habits of water creatures and things

Activities and Directions

- *This music is called "The Aquarium." What does the word "aquarium" make you think of?* (water, fish, food, water plants, snails)
- Explain the word and/or discuss the life and action in an aquarium. (Observe the aquarium or picture.)
- Listen to part of the music (about two minutes).
- Discuss the music. Encourage volunteers to demonstrate the action of things in the aquarium.
- Discuss the sounds of the aquarium (air bubbles, soft swishing of the water, fish coming to the top).
- Imitate these with mouth and/or body sounds.
- Children choose what they want to be (fish, plant, rock, etc.) in the musical aquarium.
- Children take their places where they have room to move.
- Children act out their chosen roles as they listen to the music.
- To terminate the activity the children may sit down (be rocks or sleeping fish) when tired and continue listening to the end of the piece, or, the recording may be stopped with a fade-out.
- *You were a part of water music.*

Continuing Lessons

- Relate to the lesson "The Goldfish."

- Follow the same general lesson plan for other selected parts of *The Carnival of the Animals* (Royal March of the Lion; Hens and Cocks; Fleet-Footed Animals; Turtles; The Elephant; Kangaroos; Long-Eared Personages; Aviary; Cuckoo in the Deep Woods)

THE FLIGHT OF THE BUMBLE BEE
by Nicolay Rimsky-Korsakoff
(Russia: 1844–1908)

Materials

- Bowmar Orchestral Library (Nature and Make Believe) no. 52

Pre-planning

- When you listen to this short piece notice how it stays in a limited middle register and moves quickly and constantly in downward half steps. The violins and flutes predominate.

Activities and Directions

- *What kind of a sound does a bumble bee make?*
- Take time for sounds and a discussion of bees.
- Play the piece.
- *How does the bee move?* (flies around, down, up, etc.)
- Play the piece again while children accompany with buzzing and hand motions.
- *Mosquitos hum but bumblebees . . .!* (buzz)

THE SNOW IS DANCING
from *The Children's Corner*
by Claude Debussy
(written for his daughter, Chouchou) (1908)
(France: 1862–1918)

Materials

- Recording (orchestral arrangement) Bowmar Orchestral Library no. 76 or score for piano

Pre-planning

- Listen to the soft staccato accompaniment and thin but sustained melody over it. Anticipate light finger movements and tiptoeing.

Musical Focus

- Hand dancing; free descriptive foot dancing

Activities and Directions

- *How does the snow fall?* (softly, in flakes, slowly)
- Encourage the use of the hands to demonstrate.
- Discuss the children's experiences in the snow.
- Play the piece for hand dancing.
- Discuss the hand movements and the rhythm.
- *Your hands danced like snow flakes with the music.*

Continuing Lessons

- Play the piece for foot dancing.
- Develop lessons in movement, dramatic play or quiet listening with other piece from this suite: "Jimbo's Lullay" (elephant), "Serenade for the Doll," "The Little Shepherd," "Golliwogg's Cake-walk."

THE ENTERTAINER
by Scott Joplin
(America: 1868–1917)

Materials

- Recording *Scott Joplin Piano Rags*, Nonesuch H-71248

Pre-planning

- Although there are four distinct parts in the piece (ABACD), the syncopate rhythm patterns are very much the same throughout. The first part is the only part repeated. All or part of the piece may be used. Listen to the piece several times to familiarize yourself with the basic rhythm.

Musical Focus

- Free movement to a constant syncopated rhythm

Activities and Directions

- *This kind of music makes you want to dance all over.*
- Play the first part of the piece.
- Exchange ideas about the dancing.
- Play part or all of the recording for volunteers to dance. Children may take turns dancing.
- Point out some of the characteristic movements that evolve.
- *Some kinds of music are for singing, some for listening, but this music is for dancing.*

STARS AND STRIPES FOREVER
by John Philip Sousa
(America: 1852–1932)

Materials

- Recording (Bowmar Orchestral Library no. 67)

Pre-planning

- This is probably the best loved and most famous of all American marches. It begins with a short introduction followed by the A part which is repeated. A contrasting part follows A and precedes the Trio which on some recordings has a chorus.

Musical Focus

- Listening to a band (winds and percussion instruments)
- Marching to music

Activities and Directions

- *Sometimes we call our flag "The Stars and Stripes." John Philip Sousa wrote this band piece to honor our flag.*
- Discuss the flag design, the way we honor it, etc.
- Play the first part of the piece.
- *This piece is played by a band. What is a band? Who has heard a band?*

- Discuss the children's experiences and what a band is.
- Have the children stand, ready to march.
- Play the piece again and lead the children in a single file, adapting the route to the available space.
- Your marching was like a parade.

Continuing Lesson

- Relate to "The American Flag," Part 5.

Guide for Using Currently Popular Songs in the Kindergarten

New popular songs are constantly being introduced; styles of singing and kinds of instrumental combinations change. In the fast moving spectrum of currently popular music, there are generally one or two songs that are suitable for children. Often these are the best and longest lasting.

These songs have certain characteristics in common: (1) distinctive rhythm, suggesting movement (but never frenzied); (2) melody in a limited range (not too high), and generally with one phrase repeated or returning; (3) lyrics that children can relate to. These may be *funny* (nonsense syllables or describing a ridiculous situation); descriptive of something, somebody or an experience with which they are *familiar;* or *beautiful* in a poetic or descriptive way.

Carefully chosen popular music is one more kind of music to include in the multi-faceted musical experience of kindergarten children.

Developing the Lesson

Materials

- Recording or tape and/or musical score

Pre-planning

- Listen to the recording or play through the score to evaluate.

Musical Focus

- Determine the focus according to the strengths of the composition—lyrics, melody, rhythm, occasion and/or season.

   Lyrics: Children love to sing the new songs brought into their homes by siblings or heard on radio or television. New songs with appropriate lyrics establish a tie between home and school.

   Melody without words: occasionally, a new popular song will have inappropriate lyrics but a dynamic and attractive melody.

In this case use an instrumental arrangement of the composition.

Rhythm: The rhythm of most new songs is duple with an underlying even beat and a melody with its own rhythmic overlay. Only occasionally is there a deviation from this pattern into a triple meter.

Background music: Some popular songs are effective in establishing special moods like calm, thoughtful or exciting, stimulating. Use them during rest periods, painting or craft activities or play periods, according to the mood to be established.

Activities and Directions

- *This is a new song. Have you heard it someplace?*
- Play the recording and lead a discussion of the song.
- Develop the focal point of the lesson.

  Sing the lyrics: Read and discuss the lyrics. Lead the learning of key phrases.

  Moving to the music: Outline traffic and plans for free or directed movement.

  Listening: May be inactive and quiet or active with clapping or other movement.
- *This is a good song because...*

Children involved in making music are establishing their own basic concepts of music. They move, chant, and sing, sometimes slowly, sometimes fast. They learn to sing high or low and to sing ascending and descending melodies. They begin to distinguish between even and uneven rhythms and learn to slow down or speed up. Their responses in song and movement are their first lessons in musicianship.

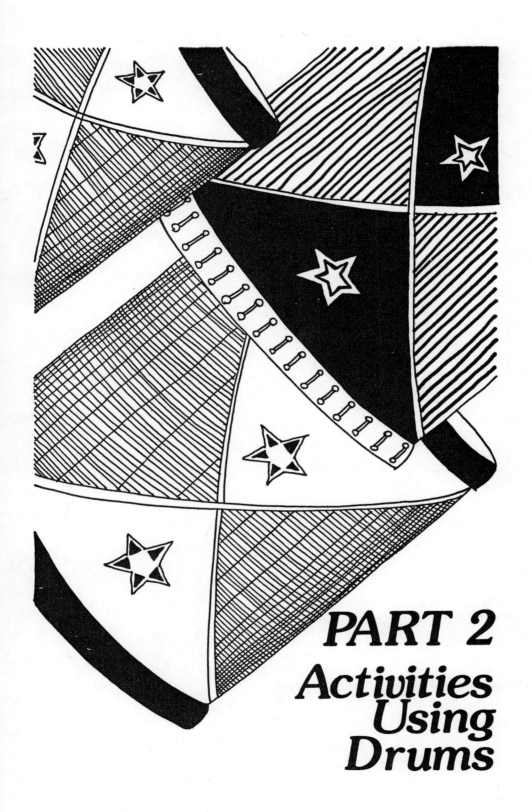

PART 2
Activities Using Drums

Part 2

ACTIVITIES USING DRUMS

♪ ♪ ♪ ♪ ♪

A drum is a major music medium for a young child. A small carrying drum, used appropriately, is an important and valuable vehicle for musical expression. Playing a drum combines effective and cognitive experiences developing motor skills and creative abilities simultaneously.

In these lessons the senses — hearing, touching, seeing — are used in the exploration of sound sensations, hand manipulation, and bodily movement. The focus is on developing awareness of the elements of music by participation. Activities always include rhythm; most of the time, melody; and occasionally, harmony. Although the development of basic concepts of rhythm is foremost, concepts of timbre, pitch and intensity are also emphasized.

♪ ♪ ♪ ♪ ♪

General Principles of Drum Sounds

Pitch (Location of the sound from high to low)

- The larger the drum, the lower the pitch.
- The sound from the center of the drum head is generally lower than the sound from near the rim. However, the smaller the drum, the less contrast there is between the sound from the center and near the rim.

Timbre (Quality of sound)

- Metal, wood, cardboard, and plastic drums have varying qualities of sounds. A small wooden drum with a stretched skin or plastic head on one end is the most typical drum found in the kindergarten. It is also one of the sturdiest.
- The timbre of handmade or adapted drums varies greatly depending on the materials.

Intensity (Degree of loudness or softness)

- The sounds of small drums are always softer than of those of large drums like tympani or the bass drum. However, the intensity of any drum may be increased or decreased by the force behind the strike on the drum head and the size and texture of the mallet. (Tapping fingers that are held close to the drum head makes a sound softer than that made by a fist swung from a distance. A padded mallet makes a sound softer than a hard rubber or wooden mallet.)

Drums in the Kindergarten

A good drum for kindergarten is (1) sturdy (will not fall apart while being played), (2) easy to hold (so a child will not drop it), (3) portable (suitable for carrying while marching, dancing), (4) made of reasonably priced, *good* materials, or adapted from sturdy available materials.

Buy

- Hand bongo with or without a thong handle
- Tom-tom (single or double head)
- Small conga
- Tunable hand drum

Make

- Stretch canvas, heavy plastic or wet skin over wooden bowl, small plastic bucket or cardboard container. (Skins shrink as they dry and make excellent heads.) Tack, tape or tie with string or elastic to secure the head.

Adapt

- Round cardboard container, preferably barrel-shaped
- Plastic jug. Hold by neck. Strike on the bottom.
- Small plastic or wooden waste basket or bucket

Mallets

- Grasped firmly near one end

Buy

- wood, felt, hard rubber, soft padded

Make

- Glue one of the following on the end of thin doweling or stick: bead, ball, cork, or covered foam.

Adapt

- wooden spoon, eraser, pencil, or rhythm stick.

Making and Playing Drums

WE MAKE OUR DRUMS

Materials

- Previously collected objects
- Prepared work areas and storage space for finished drums

Focus and Skills

- Adapting materials into improvised drums
- Decorating and individualizing drums

Activities and Directions

- *Today we are going to get our drums ready to play.*
- Each child displays his/her materials.
- Discuss each project so that everyone knows what his/her task is.
- Direct movement from one work area to the other.
- Discuss the decoration (painting cartons, pasting paper on cans, etc.) and printing of names on the drums.
- Supervise the individual work. A second adult may help.
- Have the children put the drums away.
- *Our drums will be ready to play next time.*

WE PLAY ON OUR DRUMS

Knock, knock knock, knock and knock (and knock). Knock, knock, knock, knock and knock.

Materials

- Drums made or adapted by the children

Pre-planning

- Plan an orderly distribution of the drums before the lesson, and the collection and storage of them after the lesson.
- Drums made or adapted from available materials may vary, not only in texture, but in size and shape. As a result, the way drums are held may also vary. As a guide to holding the drums, consider these factors: (1) A small drum will probably be held and played by the same child. Try grasping the edge with one hand. Hold it under one arm or between the knees. (2) A large drum may be set on a table or the floor and, if necessary, steadied with one hand.

Skills and Focus

- Holding the drums
- Exploration of playing skills (knuckle knocking, hand patting, and finger tapping) to produce a variety of sounds
- Singing and playing the drums at the same time

Activities and Directions

- *Hold your drums ready to play.* Quickly check the holding position of each drummer.
- *Let's listen to the sounds from your drums.*
- Have each child take a turn producing a sound from his/her drum.
- Demonstrate knocking, patting and tapping, using the rhythms of the new drum song. After each demonstration, let the children repeat the skill individually, then all together.
- *This is our new drum song.* Sing the song for the children.
- The children repeat the song. Correct any mistakes in singing the melody.
- Have everyone sing and knock on the drums; repeat and pat the drums; repeat and tap on the drums.
- *Playing our drums keeps time for our singing.*

Continuing Lessons

- Move, sing and play.

KNOCK ON THE DRUM

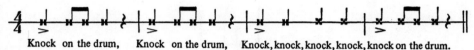

Knock on the drum,   Knock on the drum,   Knock, knock, knock, knock, knock on the drum.

Materials

- One or more drums

Skills

- Holding the drum firmly under one arm and striking it with the fist

Musical Focus

- Producing a vigorous rhythm and strong accents on the drum
- Feeling the rhythmic vibrations through body contact with the drum

Activities and Directions

- *Fists make good drum knockers. Make your hands into fists. (How do you make a fist?)*
- Move both fists in rhythm as you say the chant. Have the children imitate this.
- With the children, repeat the chanting and knocking, first with the right fist, then with the left. (Check right and left.)
- Hold the drum under the *left* arm; beat out the chant with the *right* fist. The children imitate this using their drums or imaginary drums.
- Hold the drum under the *right* arm; beat out the chant with the *left* fist. Have the children imitate this.

- The children take turns holding and beating out the rhythm. (Each child chooses the natural right or left position.)
- *A fist knocker makes a sharp, strong sound.*
- End with all beating out the chant, exaggerating the accents.

Continuing Lesson

- Use the fist technique with a familiar song.

PAT THE DRUM BOX

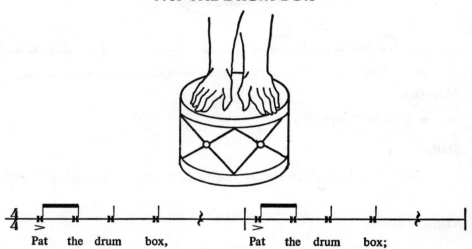

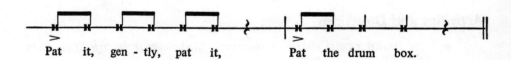

Pat the drum box,   Pat the drum box;

Pat it, gen - tly, pat it,   Pat the drum box.

Materials

- One or more drums

Skills

- Holding the drum between your knees (The children may sit on the floor.)
- Using flat hands to pat the drum head center—then near the rim

Musical Focus

- Experimenting with producing and listening to rhythmic sounds

Activities and Directions

- *A drum is a box, a kind of musical box. Listen to this drum.*
- Using two hands, pat the drum center in the rhythm of the chant—but without speaking.
- Briefly discuss holding and patting the drum.
- Let the children take turns (or all pat their own drums).
- Chant as you pat the drum again.
- Have the children chant and pat their drums with you. Those without drums pat their thighs.
- Repeat the chant, all patting with the left hand.
- Repeat with the right hand.
- Repeat, alternating hands in their own way.
- *We played the rhythm of the chant on the drum(s).*
- **The lesson may end here.**
- Pat the drum in the middle. Pat it near the rim.
- Repeat as necessary and discuss the difference in sounds.
- The children take turns demonstrating the new sound.
- A volunteer (or all) accompany the chant with pats near the rim; repeat in the center.
- *We can make two sounds patting the drum head in the center and near the rim.*

Continuing Lessons

- Use the patting technique to accompany a familiar song.
- Parade to the drum storage area, chanting and playing.

I WILL LET MY FINGERS TAP

Materials

- One or more drums

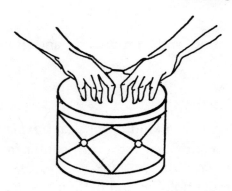

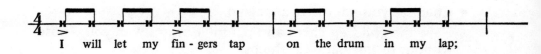

I will let my fin - gers tap   on the drum   in my lap;

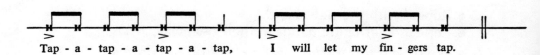

Tap - a - tap - a - tap - a - tap,   I will let my fin - gers tap.

Skills

- Tapping out a rhythm with the fingers (drum between knees, drum under one arm)

Musical Focus

- Reinforcing the duple rhythm from the "patting" and "knocking" lessons.
- Hearing the difference between the soft tapping sound and the sounds produced by patting or knocking.

Activities and Directions

- *We can play the drum with our fingers. Listen to my fingers tap on the drum.* (Tap out the chant, drum between knees.)
- Discuss the sound and the way the fingers move.
- Together, tap and chant. (Children tap on their drums or on their thighs.)
- Quickly give volunteers (or every child) an opportunity to tap out the chant.

- Repeat the chant, holding the drum under one arm.
- Have a volunteer do the "patting" chant. Let the other children imitate.
- Have a volunteer do the "knocking" chant. Let the children imitate.
- Discuss these sounds and compare them to the sounds of the tapping chant (louder or softer, sharper, etc.).
- *Tapping fingers make soft sounds on the drum.*

I'M A DRUM DRUM DRUMMER

Materials

- One or more drums

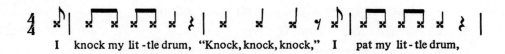

I knock my lit-tle drum, "Knock, knock, knock," I pat my lit-tle drum,

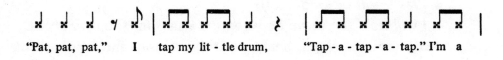

"Pat, pat, pat," I tap my lit-tle drum, "Tap-a-tap-a-tap." I'm a

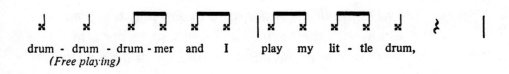

drum - drum - drum - mer and I play my lit - tle drum,
(Free playing)

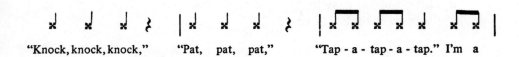

"Knock, knock, knock," "Pat, pat, pat," "Tap-a-tap-a-tap." I'm a

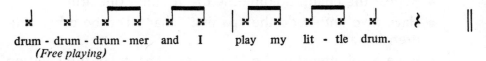

drum - drum - drum - mer   and   I | play   my   lit - tle   drum.
(Free playing)

Skills

- Three playing techniques (knocking, patting, tapping) while holding the drum in one position (between knees or under one arm).

Musical Focus

- Reinforcing the concepts of different kinds of sounds from one instrument, as well as degrees of intensity (loud to soft)

Activities and Directions

- *We can hold the drum different ways. We can play the drum different ways.*
- *Who remembers the knocking chant?* Volunteer(s) demonstrate(s) while the children chant.
- *Was it soft or loud?* (loud)
- *The patting chant?* Demonstrations and chanting.
- *Was it very soft or very loud?* (medium)
- *The tapping chant?* Demonstrations and chanting.
- *Was it soft or loud?* (soft)
- *I will hold the drum between my knees for the new chant.*
- Say the new chant, beating out the rhythm and emphasizing the differences in intensity.
- The children join in with their drums or by striking their thighs.
- *I will hold the drum under my arm and play the chant.*
- All join in with their drums or by striking upper arm.
- *We can make loud, medium or soft sounds on a drum.*

Continuing Lessons

- The children may improvise new chants with drums, choosing their own techniques.

THE JINGLE DRUM
(Tambourine)

verse 2: **Boom-da, bang-da, boom-da, bang-da, boom, bang, boom.**

Materials

- One or more tambourines

Skills

- Hold the tambourine firmly with the thumb in the thumb hole, or hold one edge with a fist, drum head facing the other hand. To shake, hold the tambourine up and turn your wrist. To strike, hit the drum head against the other fist, on the elbow or knee.

Musical Focus

- Producing two different sounds from one instrument
- Singing tongue-twisting, descriptive words to an easy tune

Activities and Directions

- *A tambourine has jingles around it and it has a drum head. Sometimes I call it a jingle drum.*
- *This is how I hold it.* Demonstrate.

- Have the children simulate the holding position.
- *This is how I sound the jingles.* Demonstrate.
- Have the children simulate the action as you play.
- Sing the first verse, keeping time by shaking the tambourine.
- Give opportunities for children to shake the tambourine as all sing the verse. Offer help with the words or playing technique as needed.
- *This is one way to play it like a drum.* Demonstrate by striking it against your fist. The children simulate the action.
- Sing the second verse and keep time by striking the tambourine against your fist.
- Give opportunities for children to strike the tambourine as all sing the second verse. Offer help with words or playing technique as needed.
- Sing the entire song with the children playing the tambourines.
- *We made two different sounds on the tambourine.*

Continuing Lessons

- Add jingle bells and a drum to emphasize the dual role of the tambourine, and also to include more children in the playing.
- Use the tambourine striking the elbow, then the knee.

Sticks and Mallets on the Drum

THE FL-IM FL-AM SONG

Fl-im, fl-am,   fl-ib - er - ty fl-am;   Fl-im, fl-am,   fl-ib - er - ty, WHAM!

Materials

- 2 drum sticks, doweling, etc.

Skills

- "Fl" is very short. It is played with the left stick.
- "Im" and "am" are played with the right stick. The "Wham" is played with both sticks.

Musical Focus

- Uneven rhythm (short-long)
- Producing this rhythm with the voice, the hands and the drum sticks

Activities and Directions

- *The fl-im fl-am song is a short-long kind of song.*

- Sing the song slowly with strong accents.
- Sing it again with the children.
- *How did you sing "Fl"?* (short)
- *How did you sing "im" and "am"?* (long)
- Together, sing it several times, keeping the short-long rhythm by patting the thighs with alternate hands in preparation for playing the drum.
- Demonstrate the left and right stick technique.
- Give opportunities for children to play the drum as others sing and pat thighs.
- *Your hands, your voices, and the drum sticks sounded the "flim flam."*

Fl-im Fl-am Games

1. "WHO" Game

Children close their eyes, heads down. Teacher chooses a drummer by touching one child on the shoulder. The chosen drummer quietly goes to the drum and plays and sings, ending the song with "Oh, guess who I am." With eyes still closed children raise hands to guess. The first successful guesser plays the drum while all sing, and also chooses the drummer for the next game.

2. "WHERE" Game

Choose a drummer. Children close eyes, head down. Drummer moves quickly and quietly to another part of the room; then plays the drum and sings, ending with "Guess where I am." The first to guess the location is the next drummer.

3. "TAKE TURNS" Game

A small drum is passed around or children line up to play a large drum. Each verse ends "Now (Robert) may WHAM!"

BANG! GOES THE DRUMMER
(Tune—Pop! Goes the Weasel)

Materials
- Padded mallet

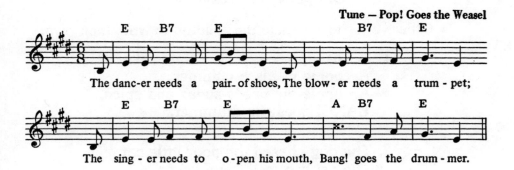

The danc-er needs a pair of shoes, The blow-er needs a trum - pet;

The sing - er needs to o - pen his mouth, Bang! goes the drum - mer.

Skills

- Hold the mallet firmly near the end.
- Precision playing. Because the drummer strikes the drum only once in the verse, he/she must be ready for the stroke.

Musical Focus

- Concentrated involvement in a strong rhythm
- Rhyming nonsense verse with humor

Activities and Directions

- *The drummer plays only one "bang" in this funny song.*
- Sing the song once, clapping or playing the drum on the "Bang!"
- *When does the drummer play?* (Bang)
- Discuss the holding of the mallet and drum.
- *How does the drummer play?* Volunteers demonstrate

- Sing the last phrase several times with everyone clapping and with a volunteer playing.
- Sing the entire song together with (a) drummer(s).
- *The drummers were ready to play the "Bang!"*

Continuing Lessons

- Traditional words:

> All around the cobbler's bench,
> The monkey chased the weasel.
> The monkey thought 'twas all in fun,
> POP! goes the weasel.

- Other verses to stimulate the children to write their own:

1. A frosting needs a chocolate cake,
   A cookie needs a yummer;
   An apple pie needs sugar and spice,
   BANG! goes the drummer.

2. The dog chased the poor little cat,
   The cat ran faster and faster.
   The drummer played and the dog ran away.
   BANG! goes the drummer.

Creative Use of Playing Skills

SPEAK DRUM SPEAK

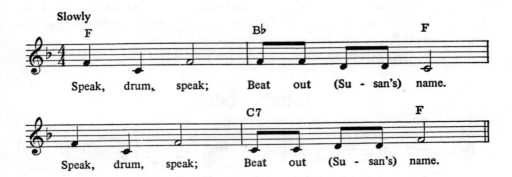

Materials

- A large drum conveniently located on the table or floor, or a small drum that can be passed from one child to another

Skills

- The drummer may use any technique already used in a previous lesson.

Musical Focus

- Developing concepts of word rhythms
- Reproducing names with drum rhythms

Activities and Directions

- *We can play the rhythms of our names on the drum.*
- Sing the song, inserting your own name. Then beat the rhythm of your name on the drum.
- Sing the song again, inserting the name of a child. Invite the child to play his/her name on the drum.
- Ask for a volunteer to play the drum. Everyone sings the song to introduce the volunteer drummer who plays the rhythm of his/her name.

- Repeat the song and name several times.
- *Different names have different rhythms.*

Continuing Lesson

- Play the rhythm of a *very* familiar song. The children guess the name of the song. Then they sing the song. A drum accompaniment with either a steady beat or the rhythm of the words completes the activity. Relate this to "The Song We Know the Best."
- Relate to "Polyrhythm Parade," Part 5.

CHUG-A-CHUG

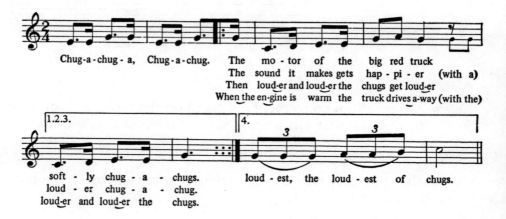

Chug-a-chug-a, Chug-a-chug. The mo-tor of the big red truck
The sound it makes gets hap-pi-er (with a)
Then loud-er and loud-er the chugs get loud-er
When the en-gine is warm the truck drives a-way (with the)

1.2.3.   4.

soft - ly chug - a - chugs.   loud - est, the loud - est of chugs.
loud - er chug - a - chug.
loud-er and loud-er the chugs.

Materials

- Any kind of a drum

Skills

- The "chug-a-chug" sounds of the introduction may be continued throughout on the drum. Use any previously learned playing technique that gives the desired sounds. The introduction is very soft. Each verse is louder (crescendo).

Musical Focus

- A small group singing and at least one drummer playing an independent part (ostinato) (chug-a-chug) while others sing the song

Activities and Directions

- *This song is about getting a big red truck started.*
- *How does a truck motor sound?* (Chug-a-chug)
- Repeat the introduction several times with the children.
- Sing the song.
- Review the words of each verse in rhythm. (Set up the sequence.) Discuss the increasing volume.
- Add the drum to the introduction. Discuss playing techniques.
- All sing the song with the drum.
- Repeat the song with two or three children singing softly and one child playing the drum part throughout.
- *This song has two parts: The "chug-a-chug" and the words that tell about the big red truck.*

Continuing Lessons

- The "chug-a-chug" may be played on the E and G bells or on the keyboard.
- Dramatize the song with the singing and playing.

THUMPETY THUM

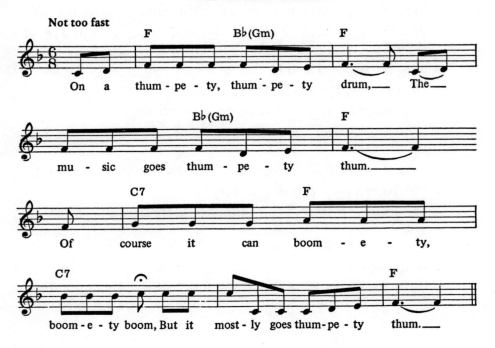

Materials

- One or two drums, one with a low pitch (for "boomety boom")

Skills

- Adapting playing skills to produce the desired sounds
- "Thumpety thum" may be played by striking the edge of the drum with flat fingers or by tapping the center with finger tips. "Boomety boom" may be played with the knuckles or flat hands. Both sounds may be played with a mallet.
- With two drummers, the sounds may be contrasted on two drums.

Musical Focus

- Contrasting sounds on the drum and describing them verbally

Activities and Directions

- *With our fingers let's play "thumpety thum."* (on the table, chair or floor)
- Repeat together "thumpety thum" until the children pick up the rhythm with their fingers.
- Sing the first 4 measures, playing thumpety thum on the drum.
- Pass the drum around for the children to play and sing several times.
- Sing measures 5 and 6.
- *How can you play "Boomety boom?"*
- Give opportunities for experimental playing.
- *Which is louder, "boomety boom" or "thumpety thum"?* Discuss.
- Sing the entire song. Repeat with (a) volunteer drummer(s).
- Everyone sings with the drummer(s).
- *"Thumpety thum" is soft and "boomety boom" is loud.*

Continuing Lesson

- Lead the children in improvising a spoken ostinato to repeat throughout the song or for the more descriptive measures.

MY YEAR

I run in fast wind;
Red, brown, yellow leaves whirling.
Autumn is chilly!

My hands catch the snow;
White flakes quietly tumbling.
Wintertime is cold!

I walk through showers;
Tulips, daffodils showing.
Springtime is warm!

I skip in sunshine;
Daisies, roses, weeds growing.
Summertime is hot!

Skills

- No even beat is suggested in the words of this Haiku. All drum sounds are subdued and are in the background for the reading of the verses. The drummer may announce each season with a fanfare. If the drummer is moving he/she may hold the drum under one arm.
- Suggested drum playing: Autumn: Bounce the finger tips in quick succession throughout the verse. Winter: Move the fingers quietly in circles on the drum head. Spring: Beat a soft even walking rhythm with knuckles or mallet. Summer: Tap the rim of the drum with a pencil or narrow dowel. Use the rhythm, long-short.
- The reading of the Haiku should be relaxed but descriptive, with inflection and tone of voice communicating the drama of the words.

Musical Focus

- Accompanying the verses with appropriate drum sounds
- Dramatizing the verses with rhythmic action. Some suggested actions are: Autumn: Run on tiptoe, whirl or indicate whirling leaves with hands; indicate feeling chilly. Winter: Hold out

hands to catch flakes, indicate tumbling with the hands; show how you feel cold. Spring: Walk in rhythm, stoop to the floor to see the bulbs; indicate being warm. Summer: Skip, show how flowers grow; indicate being hot.

Activities and Directions

- *The weather changes with the seasons of the year. Now it is (autumn).*
- Read the (autumn) verse.
- Read it line by line and discuss the descriptive words. Invite suggestions for action.
- Read the verse again encouraging the children to move with the words. (The suggested actions may be used instead.)
- Read the verse encouraging the children to say it with you as they move. Accompany the movement with the drum. Show the children how you played.
- Tell the children to repeat the words and actions with a volunteer drummer.
- *We described what happens in the (autumn).*

Continuing Lessons

- All verses may be introduced at the same lesson or they may be introduced separately in the appropriate season.
- When preparing this activity for a program, use the suggestions of the children as much as possible. The children may recite the verses in unison. Be definite about decisions. Rehearse the routine exactly the same each time after the decisions have been made. Artwork such as paper leaves and snowflakes may be incorporated into the action.
- Relate to "The Season Chant" or one of the seasonable songs in Part 5.

Mini-Stories with the Drum

THE BIG, NOISY GIANT AND THE LITTLE, QUIET PONY

The big, noisy giant chased the little, quiet pony across the meadow. The big, noisy giant walked, "Lou, lou, loud; lou, lou, loud." The little, quiet pony ran as fast as he could, "Sof, sof, soft; sof, sof, soft." Just as the pony reached the barn door, the giant caught up with him "Lou, lou, loud; lou, lou, loud," and leaned over to grab the little, quiet pony.

But the farmer inside the barn heard the big, noisy giant "Lou, lou, loud; lou, lou, loud," and opened the door just wide enough for the little, quiet pony to run in "Sof, sof, soft; sof, sof, soft." Then the farmer closed the door and locked it.

The big, noisy giant was furious and yelled and yelled as he walked "Lou, lou, loud; lou, lou, loud" back across the meadow and over the hill.

And for a long time the little, quiet pony stood close to the farmer in the barn.

Materials

- One or two drums

Skills

- Review of playing skills to produce loud and soft sounds on the drum

Focus

- Loud and soft drum sounds in a dramatization

Activities and Directions

- *In this little story we use the drum to make loud and soft sounds.*
- *The big, noisy giant walked, "Lou, lou, loud; lou, lou, loud."*
- *Volunteer drummers demonstrate.*
- *The little, quiet pony ran "Sof, sof, soft; sof, sof, soft."*

- Volunteer drummers demonstrate.
- Tell the story with the help of one or two drummers.
- *Shall we tell the story again with new drummers?*

A RAIN STORM
(Combine activities A and B to complete the rainstorm episode.)

Activity A: THUNDER

Intro: It is cloudy. The rain is coming. Suddenly,

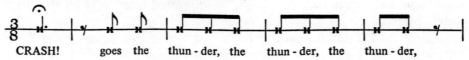

CRASH!   goes the   thun - der, the   thun - der, the   thun - der,

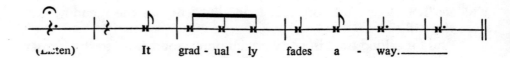

(Listen)   It   grad - ual - ly   fades   a - way._____

Materials

- The largest drum available (The larger the drum, the louder the crash and the longer the reverberation)
- Padded mallet

Skills

- Experimentation with playing techniques on available drums to produce the required sound

Musical Focus

- Directed listening (the impact of a sudden sound with its gradual dying away—called diminuendo or descrescendo)

Activities and Directions

- *Sometimes when a rain storm is coming you can hear the thunder.*

- *How does it sound?* (loud, sharp). Some children may have heard thunder and want to tell about it.
- *How can we make the sound of thunder on the drum?* Volunteers demonstrate.
- Speak the introduction and sing-song the chant. Put one hand to your ear to listen; end softly.
- Repeat with the help of a volunteer drummer.
- Discuss the effects described in the chant and drumming.
- Everyone repeats the chant together with another volunteer drummer.
- *The crash was loud but gradually the sound became softer.*

Activity B: The RAIN

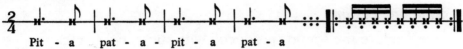

Intro: The rain is here.

Pit - a   pat - a - pit - a   pat - a

Materials

- Any kind of a drum

Skills

- Finger tapping on a drum head, rim or side. Other children may tap on lap, table, chair or floor. The taps may be without any formal direction from the teacher. However, for a lesson in finger coordination, children may use index fingers first time and add a finger on each repeat. The sound will increase in volume.

Musical Focus

- Developing the concept of sound growing louder (crescendo)
- Physically experiencing the increase in volume by finger tapping

Activities and Directions

- *The rain is beginning. There are only a few drops.*
- *Let's make rain sounds with our fingers.* Lead the tapping.

- Sing the chant *once,* using index fingers on a drum.
- Have the children repeat and tap with index fingers.
- **If finger coordination is not to be emphasized, skip the next four steps.**
- Sing the chant again using two fingers on the drum. Have the children join in.
- Sing the chant again using three fingers. Have the children imitate you.
- Sing the chant again using four fingers. Have the children imitate you.
- Add the loud ending, using all fingers.
- Direct the entire chant, using a volunteer drummer. Emphasize a soft beginning and the increase in volume.
- *As the rain increased the sound became louder.*

Continuing Lesson

- Explore the sounds produced with sticks, twigs, etc.

♪ ♪ ♪ ♪ ♪

MARTA'S LITTLE RED DRUM

Marta had a little red drum which she carried under one arm. She beat the drum as she marched along, "Step, step, step, step; step, step, step, —."

Marta wanted to march in a parade but it wasn't the Fourth of July or New Year's Day or any other special day. It was just an ordinary day. But she played the little red drum anyway, "Step, step, step, step; step, step, step, —."

Sometimes she skipped and played her drum to match, "Skip ..., skip ..., skip ..., skip ...."

When she jumped, she hit the drum in between jumps, "Boom." And when she met anyone she knew she made the drum say, "Hello, hello, hello."

But most of the time Marta marched along as if she were in a parade, "Step, step, step, step; step, step, step, —." She played the little red drum every day until she was the best drummer and marcher in the neighborhood.

One day she heard there was going to be a children's parade.

And, what do you think? They chose Marta to lead the parade.

Marta played the little red drum as she marched at the front of the parade, "Step, step, step, step; step, step, step,—."

When she played "Skip ..., skip ..., skip ..., skip," the children followed Skip ..., skip ..., skip ..., skip. And when she jumped, the other children jumped and waited for the "Boom."

As the parade passed Marta's home she made the drum say, "Hello, hello, hello." And her mother waved to her.

Finally, the parade disappeared around the corner but you could still hear the sound of Marta's drum "Step, step, step, step; step, step, step,—." farther and farther and farther away and softer and softer and softer "Step."

♪ ♪ ♪ ♪ ♪

THE LITTLE OLD LADY AND THE DRUMMER BOYS

While the little old lady waited for her drummer boy, she sat in her rocking chair and did a "Rock, rock, rocking and a rock, rock, rock, rest; Rock, rock, rocking and a rock, rock, rock,—."

After awhile she heard a soft sound at the door. So she called out, "Who's there?" And a voice answered, "I'm your drummer boy. Listen to me play, "Tap, tap and tap,—, Tap, tap and tap,—; Tap, tap and tap,—, Tap, tap and tap——."

But the little old lady said, "You are not my drummer boy. He plays much, much louder." And she did a "Rock, etc."

Soon she heard a little louder sound at the door. So she called out, "Who's there?" And a voice answered, "I'm your drummer boy, Listen to me play, "Pat, pat, pat, pat, Pat, pat, pat,—; Pat, pat, pat, pat, Pat, pat, pat,—."

But again, the little old lady said, "You are not my drummer boy. He plays much louder." And she did a "Rock, etc."

Then she heard a loud sound at the door. So she called out, "Who's there?" And a voice answered, "I'm your drummer boy. Listen to me play, "Knock, knock, —, —, Knock, knock, —, —; Knock, knock, —, —, Knock knock, —, —."

But, just as before, the little old lady said, "You are not my drummer boy. He plays louder than that." And she did a "Rock, etc."

After a long time, she heard a very loud sound at the door. Once more she called out, "Who's there?"

And a voice answered, "I'm your drummer boy. Listen to me

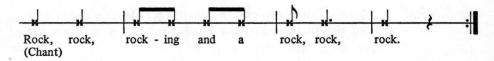

Rock,   rock,   rock - ing   and   a   rock, rock,   rock.
(Chant)

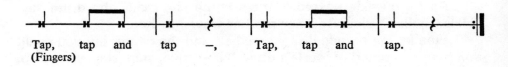

Tap,   tap   and   tap   —,   Tap,   tap   and   tap.
(Fingers)

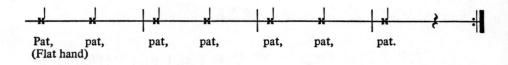

Pat,   pat,   pat,   pat,   pat,   pat,   pat.
(Flat hand)

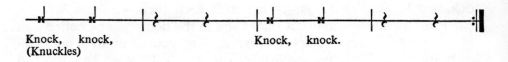

Knock,   knock,   Knock,   knock.
(Knuckles)

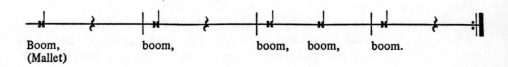

Boom,   boom,   boom,   boom,   boom.
(Mallet)

play, "Boom, — , boom, — , boom, boom, boom, — ; Boom, — , boom, — , boom, boom, boom, — ."

The little old lady thought about it for awhile; then she said, "Yes, you must be my drummer boy." And she opened the door.

There stood her drummer boy, and in back of him were three other drummer boys. The little old lady was surprised but she smiled and said, "You may all be my drummer boys." And all the drummer boys came in playing, "Boom, etc.", "Knock, etc."; "Pat, etc."; and "Tap, etc."

And the little old lady joined them with a "Rock, rock, rocking and a rock, rock, rock, — ; (Repeat softer and softer).

♪ ♪ ♪ ♪ ♪

Drum playing is an extension of the spontaneous ways children keep time. From waving, hand clapping, and game playing on the fingers to drum playing is a natural step.

Basic arm, hand and finger coordination patterns are used in beginning drumming. The forearm is used to direct the held mallet onto the drum head to sound a "Bang." The wrist is used to keep the rhythm of whole hand actions, such as patting, slapping and knocking the drum head. The fingers together or one at a time tap the drum head to make certain rhythms.

With some basic directions from the teacher on natural and practical ways to hold and play a drum, children can combine physical skills with artistic music-making.

PART 3

Activities Using Bells

Part 3

ACTIVITIES USING BELLS

♩ ♪ ♩ ♪ ♪

Bells in the Kindergarten

The clear musical tones of a ringing bell communicate varied emotions such as joy, sorrow, thankfulness, and even playfulness. Tuned bells (such as the mighty carillon), the many kinds of steel or wooden bells struck with mallets, and hand-held bells ring out melodies. Cymbals from the largest symphonic pairs of finest steel to the tiniest discs clapped with the fingers, accent the music. Triangles of various sizes can add a sharp but delicate beat. Jingle bells, possibly because of their association with sleigh bells, shake out playful, happy sounds.

In the kindergarten where the basic elements of music are introduced as a foundation for understanding all the music to come, bells are important instruments. Children not only express their emotions with bells, but also learn to distinguish the differences in bell sounds and to identify timbres. Playing and listening to various kinds of bells help children discriminate between pitches (high-low) as they notice the sizes and shapes of bells. They produce loud or soft, long and short sounds on bells. Their music, whether focused on melody, rhythm or harmony, is enhanced by bells. Bells supply music for dancing or acting out and produce sound effects for stories and accompaniments for singing. Children are naturally attracted to bells and are enthusiastic about learning how to play them in order to produce the best musical sounds.

♪ ♪ ♪ ♪ ♪

Jingle Bells

To Buy

- Bracelets, jingle sticks

To Make

- Sew jingle bells on strong tape or elastic for bracelets or on corners of small scarves for waving or swinging.
- A single jingle bell on a safety pin for shoes or pant legs

121

To Play

(Small jingle bells produce softer sounds than large jingle bells.)

- Hold by the tape or handle to allow the jingles to vibrate freely. Shake with a turn of the wrist.
- If worn on the person, move constantly in rhythm.
- To stop the sound, cup the jingles in your hands or lap—or hold them perfectly still.

Triangles

To Buy

- Four-, six- or eight-inch triangles are small enough for a child to hold comfortably.

To Adapt

- Large metal spoon or small metal cup suspended by a two- or three-inch string. Use a small spoon or heavy nail as a striker.

To Play

- Always hold by the handle or string so that the metal can vibrate freely. Hold the striker near one end. (Some strikers have a circle on the holding end.) Strike it on the solid side either inside or out. To trill quickly, move the striker from side to side.

Cymbals

To Buy

- Four- or five-inch cymbals and metal striker. Cymbals with knobs are easier to hold than ones with thong handles.

To Adapt

- Small matched pot lids with knobs

To Play

- One cymbal: Hold it by the handle or strap with one hand. With a wooden or metal striker in the other hand, strike the edge of the cymbal. (Wood and metal strikers produce different sounds.)

- Two cymbals: Hold cymbals by the knobs or straps and clap together. (Challenging: Move one cymbal up and one down, striking their edges as they pass.)

Hand Bells

Hand bells range from small plastic toy bells to large sets of chromatically tuned bells of finely tempered metal made especially for professional hand bell choirs. In the kindergarten any kind of hand bells may be used for exploring pitch and timbre. Metal and plastic are the most common.

To Buy

- Set of bells tuned diatonically to a major scale or chromatically in half steps
- Single bells of contrasting sizes—of the best quality the budget allows

To Collect

- Sturdy bells of different sizes and materials

To Play

- To produce a musical, ringing sound, hold the handle firmly and swing with the wrist so that the clapper alternately hits opposite sides of the bell.
- Tuned bells may be used to play short simple melodies.
- A bell with the clapper removed (traditionally a cow bell) is held by the handle and struck with a stick or mallet. Wood and metal produce slightly different sounds. Select the "clang" you like better.

Mallet (Bar) Bells

Mallet bells have metal bars tuned and arranged in half-steps like the middle of a piano keyboard. The bars are struck with a hard rubber or wooden mallet to produce the tone.

One kind of mallet bells, called resonator bells, is a set of detached bells. Each bar is mounted on a hollow wood or plastic block that serves as a resonating chamber. They are generally made of fine steel and have a beautiful ringing sound. They are available in one-

and-a-half octave range beginning on middle C or a two-octave range beginning on G below middle C. Extra bells may be purchased separately. They may be played as a complete instrument or one bell may be held in one hand and struck with a mallet.

Attached bells are called by various names such as tone bells, song bells or melody bells. They are mounted on a frame and are available in several sizes, most of them beginning on middle C. Some small bell sets have only the C major scale. The Orff Schulwerk mallet instruments are available in wood (xylophones) and metal (metallophones) with removable bars and are mounted on frames.

Step bells are mounted on a stair-like frame and contain the C major scale only.

To Play

- Hold the mallet firmly near one end and bounce on the center of the bar.

Bells That Jingle

MOVE
(A chant-song with movement)

One little girl had jingles in her hands; (on her wrist)
The other little girls said, "MOVE."
So the one little girl with the jingles in her hand
Moved "Jingle, jingle, jingle 'round the room."

One little boy had jingles on his feet;
The other little boys said, "MOVE."
So the one little boy with the jingles on his feet
Moved "Jingle, jingle, jingle 'round the room."

Jin - gle,   jin - gle,   jin - gle 'round   the   room.

(Repeat until the child has circled the room.)

Materials

- One or more jingle bracelets

Musical Focus

- Moving and playing the jingles in rhythm
- Individual performance before peers

Activities and Directions

- *These bells jingle when they are moved.*

- Demonstrate exactly how they are to be played by the girls.
- Say the first verse using the bells.
- *How can the little girl make the bells jingle as she moves?* (Skip, jump, move her arm, etc.)
- Choose one girl to hold the jingles etc.
- Have the other girls join in on chant and song fragment.
- Say the second verse.
- *How can the little boy make the bells jingle?* (Put bracelet on ankle or pin on shoe etc.)
- Choose one boy to hold the jingles, etc. Other boys join in on chant and song fragment.
- As time permits let other children (alternating girls and boys) act out the chant song.
- *We made the jingle bells keep time for us as we moved.*

Continuing Lessons

- *Using the same chant-song, encourage the children to explore other ways to jingle the bells. (On a stick, on the head, around the waist, in a pocket, etc.)*

JINGLES AND TINGLES

1. Wear it like a crown,
   A round, jingle crown.
   Turn your head carefully,
   But don't look down.

2. Wear it on your arm,
   And move it up and down.
   Up and down and all around,
   Move it up and down.

3. Sit and stretch your feet,
   Then put them through the jingles.
   Shake and shake and shake and shake,
   Until you get the tingles.

Materials

- Verse 1—A jingle crown may be a headless tambourine, a jingle bracelet or any other jingles that can be balanced on the head.

- Verse 2—Use bracelet or other circle jingles.
- Verse 3—Use bracelet jingles, one on each foot, or a headless tambourine or handmade jingle belt for both feet.

Musical Focus

- Learning a rhythmic activity to stimulate individual creative play
- Developing awareness of how the performer is the one who controls the instrument

Activities and Directions

- *If you are careful you can wear jingle bells like a crown on your head.*
- Demonstrate and say the first verse of the rhyme.
- *What will happen if I look down?*
- Give one or two children the opportunity to act it out as all join in on the rhyme.
- Say the second verse once, then let one or two children act it out as before.
- Say the third verse.
- *What kind of jingles can we use for this verse?* Discuss this as you display all available jingle bell materials. Let some children offer their suggestions and demonstrations.
- One child acts it out as all repeat the chant.
- *You can make the jingle bells jingle on your head, on your arm or on your feet.*

Continuing Activities

- Make jingle bells available for free play and experimentation.

ONE JINGLE, TWO JINGLES, THREE JINGLES
(Pass the Jingles)

Big jingles,
Middle jingles,
Little jingles, too.

> **Loud jingles,**
> **Other jingles,**
> **Soft jingles. Who?**
>
> **One jingle,**
> **Two jingles,**
> **Three jingles. You!**

Materials

- Three sets of jingle bells—large, medium, small (bracelets, sticks or other)

Musical Focus

- Developing the concept of the larger the instrument the louder the sound
- Providing the opportunity for every child to listen to these variations in sound and to participate in producing them (This is very discriminating listening.)

Pre-planning

- Determine the space needed for dancing. This will be influenced by the number of available jingle bells and, consequently, the number of children dancing at the same time.

Activities and Directions

- *Big jingle bells make a louder sound than little jingle bells.*
- Shake the big bells, then the little bells.
- Discuss the appearance and sound of the bells. (Note the children's remarks about size.)
- *Jingle bells that are neither big nor little make a medium sound. They are in the middle.*
- Shake the medium sized bells for listening.
- Give the three sets of bells to three children.
- Say line one. The child shakes the big jingles.
- Say line two. The child shakes the middle jingles.
- Say line three. The child shakes the little jingles.
- Slowly repeat the rhyme one line at a time, waiting for each response.

- On the word "You!" in the last line each child gives his/her jingles to another child. Repeat the rhyme until each child has had an opportunity to participate. (Each time it will be easier and probably faster.)
- *Big jingle bells make a loud sound. Bells in the middle make a medium sound. Little jingle bells make a soft sound.*

Continuing Activities

- Individual exploration of the three sizes of bells is an important factor in developing the concept of instrument size and its related volume. Make the bells available at appropriate times.
- Exploration by able children may bring out the fact that the larger bells have a lower sound. The first verse may be read, "Low jingles, Medium jingles, High jingles, too." A lesson may be developed to consider pitch instead of volume.

DANCE AND JINGLE

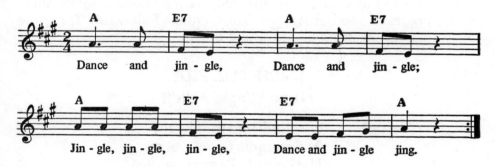

Materials

- Any kind of jingle bells (hand jingles; jingle sticks, clogs, belts, bracelets, harnesses; or headless tambourines).

Musical Focus

- Expressing joy through music participation (dancing and playing bells)

Activities and Directions

- *We can carry the jingles bells as we dance.*
- Sing the song once through.

- Ask for a volunteer to dance and play the bells as you sing it again (with the children).
- Add one child and one set of bells on each repeat until all available bells are in use. (Direct traffic as pre-planned.)
- Repeat this with another group of children until all have had an opportunity to dance.
- *Dancing and playing the jingle bells make us feel happy.*

Variations and Continuing Activities

- With one set of bells: One child dances through the song, then hands the bells to another child as the song is repeated. This may continue any number of times.
- When all children have jingle bells: Children follow a leader in a jingle bell parade. (Pre-plan the traffic route.)
- In a small specified area, one child at a time may hop and jingle the bells.
- Answering game: Start with all the children standing. One person sings and jingles the bells. When finished he/she gives jingles to another and sits down. Others follow suit. The game is finished when all are sitting down.

JINGLE BELL RIDE
(Tune "Jingle Bells")

Verse 1.   We climb into the sleigh,
              And snuggle to get warm.
              The jingle bells are jingling
              As we ride out to the farm. (Repeat.)

Chorus.   Jingle bells, jingle bells,
              Jingle all the way.
              Oh, what fun it is to ride
              In a one horse open sleigh. (Repeat.)

Verse 2.   The horse is pulling, pulling,
              The sleigh just slides along.
              The bells on horses' harness
              Are jingling out a song. (Repeat.)

Chorus.   Jingle bells, etc.

Verse 3.   Snow is white, so white;
It's frosty here and there.
The horses hooves are crunching snow,
And bells ring everywhere. (Repeat.)

Chorus.   Jingle bells, etc.

Materials

- Any number and any type of jingle bells

Musical Focus

- Keeping the beat with jingle bells
- Establishing a mental picture with the words of a song

Activities and Directions

- *The jingle bells are on the horses' harness. They play the rhythm of the horses' hooves.*
- Hand out the jingle bells. Instruct the children to cup them in their laps to keep them still.
- Read or sing the verses. Have the children keep time with the jingle bells on each chorus.
- Talk about the picture the song brings to mind. Encourage the children to talk about their experiences in the snow, and with a sleigh or sled.
- Repeat the song story, using new jingle bell players.
- *This is a wintertime song.*

Continuing Lesson

- Dramatize the song, building a tableau.

Triangles

THE FIRST STAR IS LUCKY

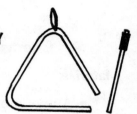

Materials

- One or more triangles or substitutes

Musical Focus

- Producing musical sound by striking metal on metal
- Chanting a traditional rhyme in rhythm

Activities and Directions

- *When it's almost dark, the stars begin to show. Some people think the first star is lucky. When they see the first star they make a wish and say this rhyme:*

    Star light, star bright,
    First star I've seen tonight,
    I wish I may, I wish I might,
    Grant this wish I wish tonight.

- *Do you ever watch the stars at night?*
- *Lead a short discussion about the change from day to night and children's impressions.*
- *Say the rhyme again one line at a time with the children repeating each line.*
- *This is a triangle.* Demonstrate the way to play it.
- Give the triangle to a child to play. Check the playing technique.
- *Let's pretend we're looking at the sky. When you (the triangle player) see the first star, play the triangle. Then we will all say the rhyme and make a wish.*
- The children are quiet; then, they carry out the play action.
- If there are other triangles, distribute them and help the children with their playing techniques.
- *Let's pretend again. This time after we make our wish we will*

132

count the stars on the triangles. (Direct the counting in unison.
If some children are able to count higher than others end with
these children showing how high they can count.)
- Combine this with "Stars Shining" (Part 1).

YOU CAN TELL THE TIME

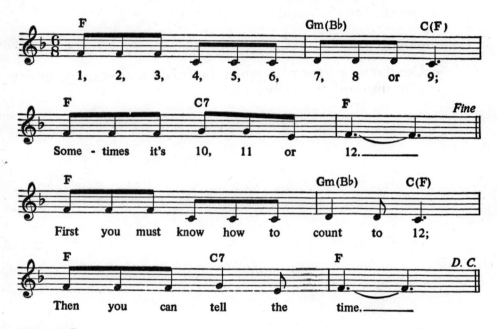

Materials

- A cardboard clock dial with a movable hour hand (or a picture
  on the chalkboard)

Musical Focus

- Singing a song that teaches a necessary skill

Activities and Directions

- (Sing slowly.) *1, 2, 3, 4, 5, 6, 7, 8, or 9; sometimes it's 10, 11 or
  12.*
- *Let's count the numbers on the clock.*
- Sing the same phrase again, this time pointing to the numbers.
  Encourage the children to sing with you.
- Repeat the same phrase with a child pointing to the numbers.

(Two or three other children may also do this.)

- Sing the next phrase of the song. Have the children repeat it.
- Move the hour hand to several numbers with children identifying the time.
- Have everyone sing the entire song with one child pointing to the numbers.
- *We sang all the numbers on the clock.*

Continuing Activity

- Use the song informally when the children are experimenting with the cardboard clock dial.

Cymbals

TINY TOES THAT TAP

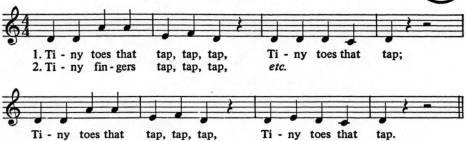

1. Ti - ny toes that   tap, tap, tap,   Ti - ny toes that   tap;
2. Ti - ny fin - gers   tap, tap, tap,   *etc.*

Ti - ny toes that   tap, tap, tap,   Ti - ny toes that   tap.

Materials

- One or more finger cymbals

Musical Focus

- Producing a soft musical sound with metal
- Matching soft, delicate movements and soft musical sounds

Activities and Directions

- *We make soft sounds when we tap our toes.*
- *Let's tap our toes and make the softest sound we can.*
- All tap. Individuals also demonstrate. (Without shoes the sound will be much softer.)
- Sing the first half of the song.
- Repeat and add the rest of the song. (Note that the second line differs from the first with only one note in measure 7.)
- Repeat line one, then line two with the children.
- Have everyone sing the entire song, tapping on each "tap."
- *Listen to the soft sound of the finger cymbals.* Play the rhythm of the words to demonstrate.
- Give the cymbals to a child.
- Sing the song again with the finger cymbals.

● *We matched soft toe tapping and soft sound on the finger cymbals.*

Continuing Lesson

● Tap with fingers, sticks, etc.

TO STRIKE A CYMBAL

Materials

● One cymbal, one striker (wood or metal)
● (Optional) A tambourine or a drum

Musical Focus

● Producing a ringing sound by striking a metal disc
● Using the cymbal to keep time for a song

Activities and Directions

● *A cymbal is a metal disc.* Ask the children to repeat this.
● Define "disc" by showing the cymbal and describing it (round and flat like a plate).
● Strike one edge of the cymbal.
● *Listen to it ring.* Strike it again.
● Give several children the opportunity to strike the cymbal.
● Review the song, "The Jingle Drum" (Part 2). Use these words, *"Tap the cymbal, hear it ring and ring, ring, ring."* (Repeat.)
● A volunteer shows how to keep time for this song. (Tap on each quarter note, the natural pulse.)
● All sing the song with cymbal accompaniment.
● (Optional) Add the tambourine on verse 1, the drum on verse 2.
● *Striking a cymbal makes a ringing sound.*

TO CLAP THE CYMBALS

The drummer plays a rum-pa-ta-tum,
The jingle bells are ringing.

The triangle sounds a ting and a ting;
Clap go the cymbals.

(Tune for "Bang! Goes the Drummer"—"Pop! Goes the Weasel" (Part 2)

Materials

- Two matching cymbals
- A drum, jingle bells and a triangle

Musical Focus

- Producing a loud, sharp ring by clapping the cymbals together
- Playing a drum, jingle bells, triangle and cymbals as directed (introducing the discipline of ensemble playing)

Activities and Directions

- *Listen as I clap the cymbals together.* (Clap them and listen until the sound is gone.)
- Allow volunteers to clap the cymbals.
- Sing the last line, "Clap go the cymbals."
- Ask for a volunteer to clap the cymbals on the word "clap" as all sing the line.
- Sing the entire verse.
- Lead a discussion about what instruments are needed and when and how to play them.
- Have four children prepare to play the instruments.
- Lead the singing and cue the playing as planned by the children. Nod your head or use your hands.
- A volunteer leads the song.
- *The clapping cymbals made a loud, sharp sound.*

Continuing Lessons

- Introduce the directing pattern "Down, up."
- Relate to the lesson "A Rain Storm" (Part 2). Use the cymbals to sound the crash of the thunder.

Hand Bells

RINGING THE BELLS

Materials

- Two or more bells including one large and one small bell (The bells may be metal, clay, plastic, or other materials.)

Musical Focus

- Arranging the bells by pitch, low-high and, in the case of several bells, in sequence from low to high

Activities and Directions

- *The bells on the (table) are of different sizes and are different shapes. Let's find out if their sounds are different.*
- Begin the exploration by ringing the largest bell. (A child may find the largest one and ring it.)
- Briefly discuss the sound and how to produce it. Give several volunteers an opportunity to ring the bell. Emphasize listening to the pitch.
- A child finds the smallest bell and rings it.
- *Which bell has a low sound?* (Large bell)
- *Listen to the smallest bell. Is it high or low?* (High)
- *Large bells make low sounds. Small bells make high sounds.*
- **The lesson may end here.**
- The children explore the sounds of the bells and arrange them by size from the largest to the smallest and listen to the difference in pitch.

Continuing Lessons and Activities

- Develop a lesson focusing on bells of different materials (metal, plastic, etc.) and their different timbres. (See "General Principles of Drum Sounds.")
- Using a set of diatonic hand bells, develop a lesson on arranging the bells into a scale; play a phrase from a familiar song.
- Use mouth sounds (bong) to imitate bells. Sing low and high pitches for large and small bells.

DANCING WITH HAND BELLS

Materials

- One hand bell for each dancer

Musical Focus

- Combining (1) chanting, (2) moving, and (3) bell ringing (Some children may dance, some may chant while others ring bells. Some children may be able to combine two or all activities.)

Activities and Directions

- Use a bell:

**I'll hold it by the handle;
I'll give my wrist a twist;
And you will hear the music of the bells.**

- All repeat the chant until a definite rhythm is established. Volunteers ring the bells.
- Volunteers (or all) dance and chant with bells.
- *The bells helped us with our dance.*

♪ ♪ ♪ ♪ ♪

THE SCHOOL BELLS AND LITTLE MATTIE

The children played in the meadow between the red schoolhouse and the deep, dark woods. After lunch the girls picked wild flowers or sat on the grass and made clover chains. Some children played tag or ran after the cottontail rabbits that hopped out of the woods.

When Miss Vernon, the teacher, stood on the porch and rang the school bell, "Bing, bing, bing," the children left the meadow and ran toward the schoolhouse. When she rang the bell, "Bing-a-ty bing, bing-a-ty bing," the children ran faster and lined up by the steps. Then Miss Vernon counted the children to be sure no one was missing.

There was a big bell hanging at the top of a pole in the schoolyard. When the rope was pulled, the bell sounded very loud, "Bong, bong, bong." Someone always rang the big bell on graduation day and other special occasions.

One spring day when the buttercups were blooming and the baby cottontails sniffed the grass at the edge of the woods, Miss Vernon rang the bell, "Bing, bing, bing." The children ran toward the schoolhouse. "Bing-ty bing, bing-a-ty bing." They ran faster.

When they were in line, Miss Vernon counted the children, "One, two—Jane and Gene, the tall twins in the eighth grade; three, four—Everett and Luther, the lively brothers; five, six—the Burton boys; seven, eight—the Gilmore girls; nine, ten—Emeline and Grace; eleven—Clarence Mack; and twelve—little Mattie who was just beginning the first grade.

But *where was* Mattie? She wasn't in line. The children looked all around the meadow but they could not find little Mattie. When Grace said she saw little Mattie chasing a baby cottontail, everyone looked toward the deep, dark woods. What if little Mattie had chased the rabbit into the woods? Who would go into the woods to find her?

Miss Vernon rang the school bell again, "Bing, bing, bing;" then, "Bing-a-ty bing, bing-a-ty bing." But little Mattie did not come running.

Everett and Luther, the lively brothers, offered to go into the deep, dark woods to look for little Mattie. Miss Vernon gave them the school bell to take with them. Perhaps little Mattie would hear the bell. Miss Vernon asked tall Jane and Gene to pull the rope and ring the big bell on the pole. The boys could hear it in the woods and follow the sound of the bell back to the meadow.

Everett and Luther disappeared into the woods, taking turns ringing the bell and calling for little Mattie. "Bing, bing, bing; Bing-a-ty bing, bing-a-ty bing." They shouted, "Little Mattie, where are you?" The big bell on the pole answered "Bong, bong, bong."

In the woods the boys heard strange animal noises and soft bird calls, but they did not hear little Mattie. The big bell sounded far away, "Bong, bong, bong."

They went farther and farther into the woods, still ringing the bell, "Bing, bing, bing; Bing-a-ty bing, bing-a-ty bing," and calling, "Little Mattie, little Mattie, where are you?" The big bell sounded faintly, "Bong, bong, bong."

Suddenly, they heard a little voice crying and sobbing, "I'm over here, over here."

The boys jumped over logs and ran as fast as they could through the darkness. A streak of sunlight broke through the treetops. And there, sitting on a cushion of moss, was little Mattie.

She looked up with tears in her eyes, and said, "The baby cotton-tail hopped away."

They could hardly hear the big bell ringing in the distance, "Bong, bong, bong."

Luther picked up little Mattie and carried her on his shoulders. As they hurried toward the edge of the woods, Everett rang the school bell as loud as he could, "Bing, bing, bing; Bing-a-ty bing, bing-a-ty bing." And the big bell on the pole answered, "Bong, bong, bong."

When they reached the meadow, everyone shouted, "Here she is. Here's little Mattie. The boys found her. Hurrah for Everett and Luther." Miss Vernon and the children gathered around little Mattie and hugged her and held her close.

Jane and Gene rang the big bell on the pole once more to celebrate, "Bong, bong, bong."

As the big bell rang out over the valley, a little cottontail rabbit hopped out of the woods and nibbled the grass. All the children stared but no one chased the rabbit.

♪ ♪ ♪ ♪ ♪

When the story is familiar, the children will enjoy helping with the bell sounds.

DANCING TO MUSIC
(A Cowbell Dance)

Materials

- A cowbell and mallet (A substitute may be any metal surface and a stick.)

Musical Focus

- Tapping a syncopated rhythm (accent on the off beat) on a cowbell
- Dancing to a syncopated beat

Activities and Directions

- *Sing all of the song, marking the word rhythm by alternately tapping hands on thighs (Patsching). Slap thighs together on "Stop!" Extend arms on "Hi!"*
- The children join you in a repeat.

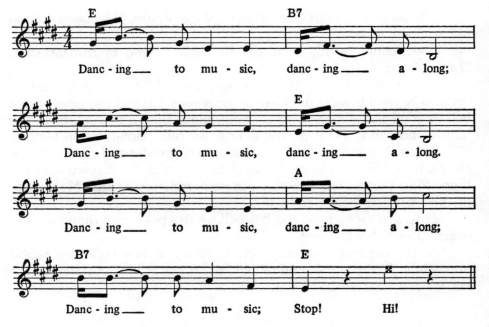

Danc - ing___ to mu - sic, danc - ing___ a - long;

Danc - ing___ to mu - sic, danc - ing___ a - long.

Danc - ing___ to mu - sic, danc - ing___ a - long;

Danc - ing___ to mu - sic; Stop! Hi!

- Sing the first phrase again, marking the word rhythm by tapping the cowbell. (Hold the mallet close to the bell.)
- Demonstrate how to hold and strike the bell and give volunteers an opportunity to tap out the first phrase.
- As one child plays the bell, the other children sing the song and patsch.
- Allow individuals or small groups to dance freely as others take turns playing the bell.
- *The bell helped us to dance.*

Continuing Lessons

- At another lesson encourage clapping, snapping fingers, moving the head, and twisting the body in the dancing. These are natural movements stimulated by the syncopation and add spirit to the dance.
- The dance may be a follow-the-leader-parade dance with the bell player in front.
- As a formal circle dance, the children may dance toward the center and back to place on alternate phrases. On the repeat the children circle right. The two actions may alternate any number of times. To end the dance lead the circle of children back to their seats.

Mallet (Bar) Bells

TWO BY TWO

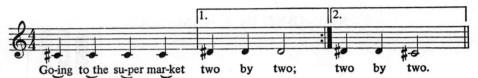

Go-ing to the su-per mar-ket two by two; two by two.

Materials

- C#, D# resonator bells and a mallet (on table or chair)
- On attached bells, mark C# and D# with colored tape or call attention to the group of black bars. The corresponding sets higher or lower may be used as an enrichment.

Musical Focus

- Developing a visual as well as aural concept to pitch
- Playing a first melody on the bells

Activities and Directions

- Sing the song indicating the two pitches with your hand(s). *Going to the supermarket, etc.*
- Sing it again with the children who also indicate the pitches.
- Demonstrate how to play the C# bell (going to the super-market); then the D# bell (two by two).
- The children sing the song as you play.
- Discuss the two pitches (higher, lower).
- Give several children the opportunity to play the bells.
- Note the ending on C#.
- *Where else could we go two by two?* (playground, school-house, etc.)
- Change the words and sing the song again with new bell players.
- *The melody we sang and the melody on the bells had the same tones.*

Continuing Lessons and Activities

- Make bells available for practice at a convenient time and place.
- One child chooses another to act out the song which is repeated until the children have circled the room.
- The same melody may be transposed higher or lower to other sets, such as CD, DE, FG, AB.

SWINGING IN A HAMMOCK

Swing - ing   in   a ham - mock,   Swing - ing side   by side.

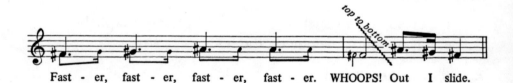

Fast - er,   fast - er,   fast - er,   fast - er.   WHOOPS! Out   I   slide.

Materials

- The melody is contained in the three-tone group of black bars (F#, G#, A#). The glissando requires the entire span of the white bars. To play the glissando hold the mallet firmly and draw across all bars from high to low. Lead the mallet with your wrist.
- Using detached resonator bells the melody may be played by one child, the glissando by another. On attached bells one child will probably play both.
- Bells and mallet should be in playing position before the lesson begins.
- (Optional) Picture of a hammock

Musical Focus

- Developing the concept of a three-tone melody (the first part of the diatonic major scale) visually and aurally
- First experiences in combining independent instrumental and vocal parts

Activities and Directions

- *We can play our new song on the bells.*
- Play and sing the first two phrases.
- Repeat the song with the children. Repeat with the bells.
- *What is a hammock?* Discuss this and show a picture if necessary.
- Give opportunity for a child to play the bells. (You may call them 1, 2, 3.) Direct the holding of the mallet.
- The child plays the bell part alone. Sing the words if this helps.
- The children sing with the bells.
- Sing the next phrase, "Faster. . . ."
- (To the bell player) "Can you play that?" Give help if needed.
- All sing this line with bell accompaniment.
- Add the glissando and ending as a surprise.
- *What happened?* Discuss the glissando and the ending.
- Help a child play the glissando. The child playing the melody plays the ending.
- Go through the song to give bell player(s) help.
- *Let's sing all of the song.*
- **Lesson may end here.**
- Other children may be given the opportunity to play.
- One or two children may act out the words, falling on the glissando.

Continuing Lessons

- "Swinging in a Hammock" may be transposed and played on any of the following three-tone combinations: CDE, C#D#E# (F), DEF#, EF#G#, FGA, GAB, G#A#B# (C), ABC#, B♭CD, BC#D#. The glissando remains the same for all combinations.

- Rotating the playing and action for groups of two (or individuals for attached bells): two children play the bells, two children act out the words. The actors become the players, two new children act out the words. This may continue as time permits.
- The song "Tip Toddle" (Part 1) may be used here as a review.

DIRECTED IMPROVISATION
(The pentatonic or five-tone scale)

Materials

- Group of three (F#, G#, A#), group of two (C#, D#) black bars arranged in order of pitch (low to high). Duplicates for more than one player may be from another set or from another octave of the same set.

Musical Focus

- The pentatonic or five-tone scale (1, 2, 3, 5, 6 of the major scale) is found in folk music on every continent. Thus, it is aptly called the universal, and sometimes, the common man's scale. Without half-step dissonances all melodic and/or harmonic combinations are pleasing to the ear.
- Improvising melodies (not necessarily remembered or recorded) on a pentatonic scale as a creative and satisfying musical experience.

Activities and Directions

- Play and sing the first phrase of "Swinging in a Hammock." *We played this song on the set of three black bars.*
- All review the entire song and teacher or a child plays the bell accompaniment.
- *What song did we play on the set of two black bars?* ("Going to the Supermarket")
- All review the entire song with bell accompaniment.
- Ask some one to play the sequence of the bells (1, 2, 3, 5, 6) up, then down.
- *Can you skip around on the bars and make a melody?* (Any phrase will be satisfactory.)

- Another child takes a turn. *Start your melody low; go higher; end low.* Allow time for the child to develop this.
- If time permits use these additional directions for other children. *Start anywhere; end high. Start high; play every bell; make up your own ending.*
- *Every day (during free period, exploring time, etc.) you may take turns making up your own music.*

Continuing Lessons

- Develop a lesson using the two lower black bars. Start with the song "I Can Stretch" (Part 3).
- Play any of these familiar songs by ear: "Japanese Rain Song" (Part 1), "Skipping Song" (Part 1), "Speak Drum, Speak" (Part 2).
- Spend one or more lessons as a period when children may "perform" their original pieces. (Pieces will vary each time they are performed. Some children may need a time limit.)

I CAN STRETCH MYSELF

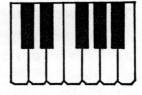

1. I can stretch my - self 'til I'm tall - er than a bear,
2. I can stretch my - self 'til I'm long - er than a snake,
3. I can puff my - self 'til I'm round - er than a ball,

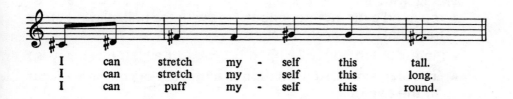

I can stretch my - self this tall.
I can stretch my - self this long.
I can puff my - self this round.

Materials

- Bars C#, D# and F#, G#, A# (resonator or attached bells), mallet

Musical Focus

- Singing a pentatonic song and playing fragments and phrases of the melody by ear

Activities and Directions

- *I can stretch myself, etc.*
- *Show me how you can stretch tall. How tall is a bear? Are you stretching taller?*
- Sing the song again with the children as they stretch.
- The children sit.
- *We will use the group of two bells (Play these.) and the group of three bells (Play these.) for this song.*
- Play the song on the bells.
- *Who would like to play "I can stretch"?* Guide the child in choosing the first bell. Sing the pitch. Help in the matching.
- *Are these the same?* Sing "I can stretch" and "til I'm tall." (Yes)
- The child plays the bells as all sing each fragment.
- *Play with us when we sing the song. How many times will we sing "I can stretch"?* (two times)
- All sing with the bell playing the fragments.
- *Let's sing with the bells and act out the words.*
- **The lesson may end here** or continue with more exploration of the melody until someone finds the entire melody.

Continuing Lessons

- Add the other two verses and any others suggested by the children.
- Sing with the bell playing "I can stretch" as an ostinato, **or** repeated pattern, throughout. Sing with the bell, playing other fragments as repeated patterns.
- Sing with the bells playing in octaves (if bell has two octaves.)
- Encourage interested children to improvise or compose pieces on the five bells.

SO STILL, SO STRAIGHT, SO TALL

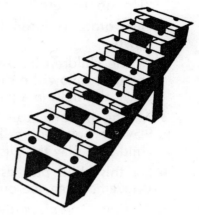

Slowly
With relaxed bell taps to complement the words.

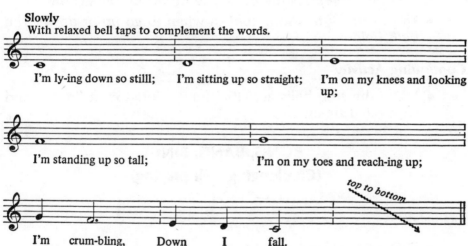

I'm ly-ing down so stilll;   I'm sitting up so straight;   I'm on my knees and looking up;

I'm standing up so tall;   I'm on my toes and reach-ing up;

top to bottom

I'm   crum-bling,   Down   I   fall.

Materials

- Step bells and mallet (Resonator or regular attached bells may be substituted.)

Musical Focus

- Developing a visual concept of rising and falling pitches
- Reinforcing the concept of aural pitch with movement

Activities and Directions

- *Each tone on the step bells is higher than the one before.*
- Play slowly from low to high.

- Offer opportunities for children to play this as the others sing "Up, up, up, etc."
- Give other children the opportunity to play both up and down.
- As the children lie on the floor, sing the song, helping the children follow the direction of the words. At the end, play down the bells in a glissando.
- All sing the song again following the directions for movement. Play the bells with at least one child watching carefully. This child may play the glissando.
- Let this child play as all sing. Direct him/her as needed. (Movement may be omitted in this word and bell practice.)
- All sing. One plays the bells, and others do the actions.
- *The words of this song told us when to go up or down. The bells helped.*

Continuing Activity

- Make the step bells available for exploration at limited and controlled times.

BONG, BANG, BING
(Challenging bell playing)

Materials

- C̲ D E F G C̄ bar bells

Musical Focus

- Playing a three-phrase diatonic melody with focus on the phrase structure.
- Relay bell playing (taking turns)
- Singing bell sounds

Activities and Directions

- *This bell song has three phrases or parts. It sounds (Sing) "Bong, etc."*
- The children repeat the first phrase with you.

Bong. bong, bong, bong, bong, bong, bong.
Alternate Verse C   D   E   D   C   C   C

Bang, bang, bang, bang, bang, bang, bang.
E   F   G   F   E   E   E

Bing, bing, bing, bing, bing, bing, bing.
G   G   G   G   C   C   C

- Play the bells for another repeat.
- Sing the second phrase with the children. (You may need to indicate pitch by hand.)
- Repeat with the bells.
- Sing the third phrase with the children.
- Repeat with the bells.
- One child plays the first phrase. Guide the child in finding the C, D, E bells. Sing along.
- All sing with the bell player.
- A second bell player investigates the second phrase with guidance from the teacher.
- All sing with the second child.
- Repeat the same steps for the third player on the third phrase.
- The three players line up ready to play.
- After playing phrase one the player hands the mallet to the next player (on the rest). The second player plays the second phrase and hands the mallet to the third player who finishes the piece.
- *Let's sing with the bell players.*

Continuing Activities

- With duplicate E and G bells the three players may play the three phrases in harmony.
- Three children who are equal to the challenge may try the piece as a round.
- The letter names may be taught as a verse.

Mixed Bells

HONEY BEAR

Hon - ey bear is a fun - ny, fun - ny bear;

He hears bells as he sits in his chair,

Hon - ey bear is a fun - ny, fun - ny bear;

Bells are ring - ing (un - der) his chair.

Materials

- Jingles, hand bell, C resonator bell or any other easy-to-carry bell

Musical Focus

- Singing a slightly syncopated melody outlining tonic and dominant chords

Special Focus

- Developing concepts of over, under, in front, in back, and to the side

Activities and Directions

- *"Honey Bear is a funny, funny bear." Do you know why? "He hears bells as he sits in his chair."*

- Sing the entire song, sitting in a chair and ringing the bells under the chair in phrases 2 and 4.
- Lead a short discussion about the song and where the children may see a bear (at the zoo, on television, in a story book).
- Lead the singing as one child sits in a chair and a second child rings the bell under the chair.
- Two other children act out the song as all sing.
- *Where else could the bells ring?*
- Two other children act out the song, this time with the bell (over) the chair.
- With the song becoming familiar and the acting out pattern set, the bell ringer may ring the bell without announcement on the second phrase and the children must fill in the correct description of the location in the last phrase.
- *We rang the bell under the chair, over the chair, etc.*

Continuing Activities

- Use this verse as an opportunity to use all available bells.

1. **All the bells a-ring-a-ring; All the bells a-ring-a-ring; All the bells a-ring-a-ring; Listen to the bells.**

HEAR THEM RING

2. **Tri-ang-le a-ting-le; Hear it ring, "Ting, ting." (_____) plays tri-ang-le; Hear it ring, "Ting, ting." Ting-a, ting-a, etc.**

3. **Listen to the tiny cymbals play, "Tn, tn." (_____) plays the cymbals; Hear them ring, "Tn, tn." Tn-a, tn-a, etc.**

4. See the cymbals clapping; Hear them ring, "Clang, clang." (_____)plays the cymbals, Hear them ring,"Clang,clang."

5. Hold the cowbell, strike it! Hear it ring, "Jang, jang." (_____) plays the cowbell; Hear it ring, Jang, jang."

6. See the mallets bouncing; Hear the bells, "Ring, ring." (E,E) (_____) bounces mallet; Hear the bells, "Ring, ring." (C,C)

7. Listen to the children play the bells, "Ring, ring." Listen to the children play the bells, "Ring, ring."

LESSON 1: LESSON USING ONE KIND OF BELL

Jingle Bells
(Triangles or cymbals may be substituted with the appropriate verse.)

Material

• All available jingle bells

Musical Focus

• Featuring a familiar instrument with a song
• Discipline of playing at the correct time, then keeping the beat for the repeated song—all to produce a musically pleasing result

Activities and Directions

• (Jimmy) *Will you play the jingle bells for us?*
• After (Jimmy) has demonstrated his ability to play the jingle bells, sing the song, directing him to play only on the "Ching, ching."
• All sing the song and (Jimmy) plays on the "Ching, ching."
• *Let's repeat the song with "Ching-a."* (Jimmy) *you keep the beat for us with the bells.*
• All sing the song with bell accompaniment.
• Offer other children the opportunity to play the jingle bells

using the same routine demonstrated by (Jimmy).

- *The first time we sang the song the jingle bells played only on "Ching, ching," but the second time we sang the song the bells played all the way through.*

Continuing Lessons

- Use other verses to feature other bells. This prepares the children for the lesson using all the bells.
- Give a series of lessons using the resonator bells. The melody is contained in the C major pentatonic scale, C D E G A. For a series of more challenging lessons, use these five bells. Introduce the lessons with verse 6. Devote at least one session to exploration, completing the melody for phrase "Hear them ring" "Ching, ching," comparing the two ways it is sung; outlining "Listen to the jing" which is the scale, completing the phrase "les" by ear. Short independent melodies using any of the bells may be composed by the children. In addition to being their own compositions, these short pieces may be used as counter melodies with the regular melody. Short fragments of the melody may be repeated throughout (ostinati).

LESSON 2: LESSON USING ALL AVAILABLE BELLS

Materials

- Jingle bells, triangles, finger and hand cymbals, cowbells and/or other hand bells, and mallet bells

Musical Focus

- Comparing the quality of sounds (timbre) of different kinds of bells
- A musical culmination of bell sounds with a review of playing techniques

Activities and Directions

- *We have several different kinds of bells.*
- Give a triangle to a child who then stands in front and demonstrates it.
- *What is the name of this bell?* (triangle)

- One at a time give out one of each kind of bell. The bell players join the triangle player in front and in turn demonstrate. Have the children name each bell.
- *Close your eyes. We are going to name the bells by listening to them. Raise your hand when you recognize the bell.*
- Without speaking, point to one bell player who plays. Call on the child whose hand was up first.
- Repeat this until all bells are guessed. (Be sure all eyes are closed.)
- Let the children briefly describe the sound of each bell and how it differs from the others.
- Hand out all available bells to the children who try out the instruments and get ready to play. Indicate quiet.
- Sing all verses. (These will be familiar from previous lessons.)
- End with every one playing on the last verse.
- *We played (six) kinds of bells.*
- Collect the bells in an orderly manner.

In these activities children have played jingle bells, triangles, finger cymbals, clapping cymbals, hand bells of various kinds and chromatically tuned mallet (bar) bells. They have developed motor skills that enable them to actively participate in instrument playing. By their participation, they have also increased their awareness of the broad scope of music making. Since bell playing is also fun, they have had a positive and happy musical experience.

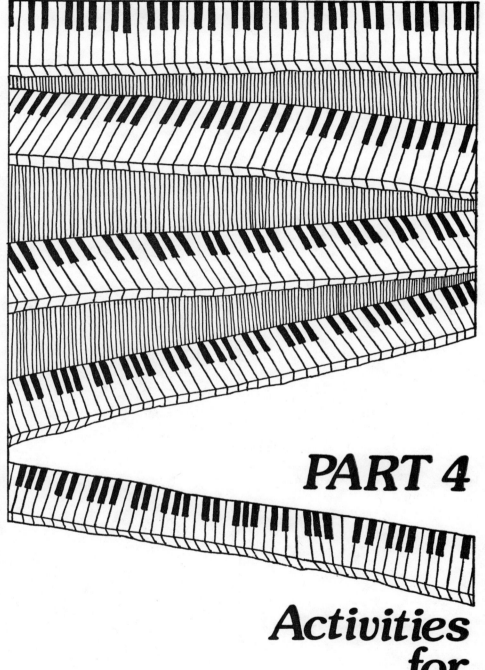

PART 4

Activities for Keyboard

Part 4

ACTIVITIES FOR KEYBOARD

♪ ♪ ♪ ♪ ♪

The lessons in Part 4 are designed to be happy, constructive and musical first experiences at the keyboard. The musical emphasis is on the continuing development of basic concepts such as high-middle-low pitches, large and small intervals, up and down melodic movement, fast and slow tempi, etc.

Motor skill emphasis is on hand movements—moving horizontally, identifying and coordinating left and right hand movements, locating specific keys with the help of the black key arrangement, using fingers independently, and generally, becoming familiar with keyboard topography.

♪ ♪ ♪ ♪ ♪

Notes About Keyboards and Lessons

1. The piano is the most commonly used keyboard. However, for these lessons most any kind of keyboard may be used. In the case of an electronic keyboard, the use of electrical switches must, of course, be supervised by the teacher.

2. Piano benches are seldom made for small children and generally have to be adapted. Ideally, a bench should be high enough for the child to play with upper arms hanging vertically and lower arms horizontally, with the keyboard. The bench may be made higher with a non-slip, stable pad.

3. The trade name of the instrument is usually printed above the middle of the keyboard. It is a good landmark for finding the middle tones.

4. To encourage individual exploration, the keyboard may be made available to children during convenient free times.

5. To expand individual exploration each child may have a desk chart, a one and a half octave cardboard keyboard. While children take turns at the keyboard other children may explore their desk charts. A desk chart helps establish a visual concept of the black and white key arrangement and personalizes the learning process.

6. During most lessons the children should have quick access to the keyboard instrument. One good arrangement is a semi-circle of chairs with nothing between the children and the instrument. They may also stand in order to see the keyboard better. In some cases children may line up to take turns.

7. It is important that every child take part in the activities at every lesson. If time does not permit every child to participate at one lesson, arrange for an informal individual experience.

Introduction to the Keyboard

HANDS ON THE KEYBOARD
(Physical preparation for playing)

Hands   on   the key - board;   Hands   on   the key - board;

Key - board,   Key - board,   Hands   on   the key - board.

Motor Skills

- Developing awareness of arm, hand, finger potentials
- How to sit comfortably at the keyboard

Musical Focus

- New sounds made by finger and keyboard contact

Activities and Directions

- (Away from the keyboard) *Stretch your arms in front of you. Bend your elbow. Look at your hands. Turn them over. Move your fingers. Make your fingers dance to our new song, 'Hands on the Keyboard.'* (Sing and make your fingers play the melody in the air. Have the children move their fingers.)
- *When we play the (piano) we sit on a bench (chair, etc.) and look at the middle of the keyboard.* (Play the song (very softly) as you sing.)
- Sing it again softly fingering the keys at random as an accompaniment.
- Give several children (all if the group is small) the opportunity to sit on the bench and finger the keys as an accompaniment for the song.
- *We sat on the bench and looked at the middle of the key-*

165

board. Our fingers made soft sounds on the keyboard as we sang.

Continuing Activities

- To be sure that every child has this experience, make the keyboard available at certain times.

SHOW ME WHERE THE MUSIC IS

Motor Skills

- Dramatizing in order to establish a routine for approaching the keyboard

Musical Focus

- Keeping time with the fingers on the keyboard

Activities and Directions

- *This is an acting out story. As I tell the story someone acts it out.* (With your help a volunteer acts out the story.)
- *In this room there is a bench.* (Point to bench.) *And on this bench there is a child.* (Sit on bench.) *And on this child there are two hands.* (Hold hands above keyboard.)

And on each hand there are five fingers. (Move fingers.) *And in these fingers there is some music.* (Finger the keys and sing.)

> **Hands on the keyboard, Hands on the keyboard;**
> **Keyboard, keyboard; Hands on the keyboard.**

- *Help me tell the story as (another child) acts it out.*
- Continue with other children.
- *We know how to sit at the keyboard and play.*

LEFT (RIGHT) HAND SONG

Motor Skills

- Left and right hand awareness
- Using one hand at a time; alternating hands

Musical Focus

- Producing an improvised melody on the keyboard

Activities and Directions

Part 1
- Sing: *This is my left (right) hand, left hand, left hand; moving fingers, moving fingers; this is my left hand.* Fit the words into the melody for "Hands on the Keyboard."
- *Hold up your left hand.* Check hands.
- Sing the song as they move their left fingers.
- Have one child go to the keyboard and prepare to play. All sing as the child acts out the words on the keyboard.
- Repeat for the right hand.
- Other children in turn repeat this as all sing.
- *We know where the left hand plays on the keyboard and where the right hand plays.*

Part 2
- Chant (2 tones, G - E): *Left hand, right hand, left hand, right hand; playing, singing, left hand, right.*
- Have one child go to the keyboard and prepare to play. Have him/her hold both hands over the keyboard. (Check left and right.)
- All chant as the child softly keeps time on the keyboard.
- Others take turns accompanying the chant.
- *We played with the left hand, then with the right hand.*

LOW, HIGH, MIDDLE

Motor Skills

- Reaching to the left and to the right on the keyboard

Musical Focus

- Part 1. Left is low.
- Part 2. Right is high.

- Part 3. The middle is neither low nor high. The singing range.

Activities and Directions

Part 1. Rumble Grumble Music
- Demonstrate. *I sit in the middle and play the lowest key. Hear it rumble; hear it grumble when I play the lowest key.*
- Discuss the sounds produced by playing the lowest keys.
- Children take turns acting out as all repeat the chant.
- *Rumble grumble music sounds low.*

Part 2. Squeak and Eek Music
- *I sit in the middle and I play the highest key. Hear it squeak and hear it eek when I play the highest key.*
- Discuss the sounds produced by playing the highest keys.
- Children take turns acting out as all repeat the chant.
- *Squeak and eek music sounds high.*

Part 3. Together in the middle
- *Left hand low and right hand high: low, high, together in the middle.*
- *Let's all act out the chant before we go to the keyboard.* (If you act it out with the children turn your back to them so that your left and right hands will correspond to theirs.)
- After several repeats, volunteers take turns acting out at the keyboard.
- *We played low and high and middle sounds on the keyboard.*

Continuing Lessons

- Kind of keyboards. Identify the kind of keyboard being used. Is it a piano? Is it full-size? Is it an organ? Are there buttons to be explained?

THE GIANT AND HIS LITTLE SISTER
(a mini-story to act out)

Motor Skills

- Establishing automatic movements toward left-low, and right-high

Musical Focus

- Establishing the concept of low-high-middle on a horizontal, plane

Activities and Directions

Once there was a giant who stepped on the low part of the keyboard and roared, "Heavy step—roar; Heavy step—roar." (Play with left hand.) The giant roared so much he fell right off the keyboard into my lap.

The giant had a little sister who was not a giant at all. She tiptoed on the high part of the keyboard. She did not roar. She said, "See me tiptoe; See me tiptoe." (Play with right hand.) The keys were too slick for the little sister and she slipped off the keyboard and fell right into my lap beside the giant.

"That is how it happened. And that is why I am holding the giant and his little sister in my lap."

Continuing Lessons

- Review the favorite lessons as an informal activity.

Black and White Keys

BLACK KEYS, WHITE KEYS, HAND GAMES

Part 1. Black Keys

Motor Skills
- Playing higher and farther back on the keyboard
- One-finger playing

Musical Focus
- Selecting and playing one key for its relative pitch

Activities and Directions
- *Some keys are black.*
- Volunteers play some black keys.
- *With one finger on your left hand pretend you are playing the lowest black key.* (All do this away from the keyboard.)
- Children take turns playing the lowest black key. (They will probably elect to play with the index finger or thumb. Any finger strong enough may be used.)
- *With <u>one</u> finger on your <u>right</u> hand pretend you are playing the highest black key.*
- Use the same routine as with left hand.
- *We played the lowest black key with one finger on the left hand and the highest black key with one finger on the right hand.*

Continuing Activities
- Play "Rumble Grumble" and "Squeak and Eek" on black keys.
- Children compose their own lowest-highest music.

Part 2. White Keys

Motor Skills
- Playing lower and to the front of the keyboard

- Continuing one-finger playing

Musical Focus

- Selecting and playing one key for its relative pitch

Activities and Directions

- *All the other keys are white.*
- Volunteers play some white keys.
- *With <u>one</u> finger on your <u>left</u> hand pretend you are playing the <u>lowest</u> <u>white</u> key.*
- Follow same routine as with black keys.

Continuing Activities

- Play "The Giant and His Little Sister" on the white keys.
- Children compose lowest-highest white key music.

Part 3. Hand Games

Motor Skills

- Changing hands from black to white keys

Musical Focus

- Producing gross sounds in groups

Easy Game

- One child sits at the keyboard. Other children play on lap, table or desk chart. With both hands the child plays some (black) keys and waits. When the teacher says, "Change" the child plays keys of the other color. The object of the game is to end on the correct color keys. To make the game more challenging, give the directions faster.

Harder Hand Game

- In this game one hand plays black keys while the other hand plays white keys. When the teacher says, "Change" the hands change to the other color keys.

Continuing Activity

- One child may give the directions and play the game alone or children may play in pairs.

SHOW ME! TELL ME!
(review game)

- *This is a "Show me! Tell me game!"*
- Children take turns at the keyboard while other children play on lap, table or desk chart.

You know . . . where to make low sounds on the keyboard.
SHOW ME!

You know . . . where to make high sounds on the keyboard.
SHOW ME!

You know . . . how to find the middle of the keyboard.
SHOW ME!

You know . . . where the black keys are.
SHOW ME!

You know . . . where the white keys are.
SHOW ME!

You know . . . where the (trade) name of your keyboard is.
TELL ME!

Black Key Groups

1—2 and 1—2—3

Motor Skills

- Locating and playing groups of 2 and 3 black keys (Playing may be with fists, fingers or flat hands.)

Musical Focus

- Playing-hearing 1—2 and 1—2—3 groups in low, middle and high registers

Activities and Directions

- Children stand around keyboard or look at full keyboard chart.
- *The black keys are arranged in groups of two (Play 1—2, groups from low to high) and groups of three. (Play 1—2—3 groups from low to high.)*
- *Let's take turns finding groups of two black keys.*
- Children line up on left of piano. Each child plays the 1—2 groups from *low to high,* then moves on. The line circles back to the left of the piano.
- *Let's take turns finding groups of three black keys.*
- Repeat the playing routine.
- *We played all the groups of two black keys and groups of three black keys.*
- The lesson may be extended so that children play the 1—2 and 1—2—3 groups from *high to low.*

PLAY-HOP GAME

Motor Skills

- Making a fist
- Moving the hands quickly horizontally from one black group to the next matching group

173

Musical Focus

- Establishing concepts of going from low to high and from high to low

Activities and Directions

- *Stretch your fingers; fold them tight. Left fist, right fist; fold them tight!*
- *This rhyme tells you how to make a fist.* Say the rhyme with the children several times, as they learn how to make a fist.
- *We play with our fists in the Play-Hop Game.*
- How to play the game:

  Stand in front of the lowest group of two (or three) black keys. (Child walks to reach other groups.) Say, "Play" as the fist plays a group. Say, "Hop" as the fist moves to the next matching group of two (or three). Continue up the keyboard. Repeat the game and play downward on the keyboard. Variations of the game: (1) When the children are in a line, one child plays up the keyboard and moves on as the next child plays. The last child to play up also plays down and others in the line follow. (2) Children may also play their own variations alone or in pairs.

TWO FINGERS ON TWO BLACK KEYS

Review "The Fingers" (Part 1)

Motor Skills

- Directed finger playing (fingers 1, 2)

Musical Focus

- Combining rhythmic speech and the playing of specific keys

Activities and Directions

- Children stand near the keyboard.
- *We can play the groups of two black keys with fingers 1—2 on the right hand.* Hold up fingers.

- Demonstrate on keyboard, using right thumb and index finger and saying, "One, two." Move from *low to high.*
- Children take turns playing and moving on. Give help when needed.
- *We can play the groups with fingers 1—2 on the left hand.* Hold up fingers.
- Demonstrate, playing from *high to low.*
- Children take turns playing and moving on.
- *We played all the groups of two black keys with two fingers.*

Continuing Activities

- Play right hand down (fingers 2—1)
- Play left hand up (fingers 2—1).
- Jingles to sing as you play:

> **One two; buckle my shoe.**
> **Birds black; fly back.**
> **Clown, down; Down, down.**

PIECES FOR THE TWO BLACK KEYS

Marching

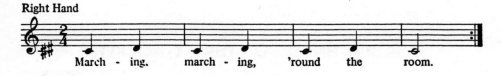

Right Hand

March - ing,   march - ing,   'round   the   room.

Left Hand

Bye   low,   bye bye low;   Sleep,   child,   sleep.

Bye Low

Motor Skills

- Playing with two fingers to match the melodic pattern

Musical Focus

- Hearing, playing, singing a melody going up and down one step

Activities and Directions

"Marching"

- *Marching is a new song.*
- Sing it once. Sing it again with the children, indicating the pitches with horizontal hand moving up or down.
- The children repeat with hand motions.
- Play it on the middle group of two black keys. Use *right* thumb and index finger (fingers 1 and 2).
- Play it again as the children sing.
- With your back to the children play it in the air so that the children may copy the finger actions.
- Two children go to the keyboard and play, one on each side of the teacher. Sing with the playing. Check fingers.
- Children take turns playing. Those waiting for a turn may play in the air. Some may march.
- *We played; we sang; we marched.*

"Bye Low"

- Follow the plan as for "Marching."
- "Bye Low" is played with the *left* thumb and index finger (fingers 1 and 2).

THREE FINGERS ON THREE BLACK KEYS

Activities and Directions

- Children stand near the keyboard.
- Review "Play-Hop Game" on *three* black keys
- *We can play the groups of three black keys with fingers one, two, three on the right hand.* Hold up fingers.

- Demonstrate, saying, "One, two, three." Move from *low to high.*
- Children take turns playing and moving on.
- *We can play the groups with fingers one, two, three on the left hand.* Hold up fingers.
- Demonstrate, saying, "One, two, three." Move from *high to low.*
- Children take turns playing and moving.
- *We played all the groups of three black keys with fingers one, two, three.*

Continuing Activities

- Play the right hand down (fingers 3—2—1)
- Play left hand up (fingers 3—2—1)
- Jingles to sing as you play:

> **One, two, three; step with me.**
> **Three black keys; straight like trees.**
> **Shiny black keys; set in threes.**
> **Going up (down); up, up, up (down).**

PIECES FOR THE THREE BLACK KEYS

Walking

(Right Hand)

Walk - ing   and   walk - ing;   Our   fin - gers   are   walk - ing.

Shells and Sand

Slowly
(Left Hand)

Sea   shells   in   sand;   Shells and sand   in my   hand.

Adapt the lessons for "Marching" and "Bye Low" to these pieces for the three black keys.

Combining the Black Key Groups

PIECES FOR 1, 2, 3 and 1, 2 BLACK KEYS

Climbing Up the Mountain

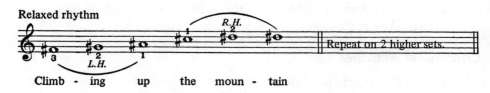

- Using familiar finger patterns in a new situation
- Awareness of changing hand and finger positions

Musical Focus

- Becoming familiar with the major pentatonic (five tone) scale

Activities and Directions

- Children may stand around the keyboard.
- *We play our new piece "Climbing Up the Mountain" on a set of three and two black keys.*
- Play "Climbing" on middle keyboard.
- Sing it. Children repeat it. Play it for singing.
- Demonstrate the left hand (Climbing up) in the air. Children copy fingers and sing. Check fingers.
- Demonstrate right hand (the mountain). Note that "moun" and "tain" are played on the same key.
- Repeat the entire piece in the air, children copying.
- Play it for singing, children playing it in the air or on desk charts.
- One child plays it on the middle keyboard, then moves to a higher set.
- Another child plays.
- A third child plays. All three play together.

178

- Other children take turns.
- *We played* <u>Climbing</u> *on the set of three and two black keys.*

Down the Mountain, Down

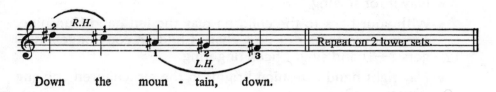

Down   the   moun - tain,   down.

- Follow the same routine as for "Climbing Up the Mountain."
- (Alternative) One child plays and moves to the other side of the keyboard. Each child plays and moves away. This is a fast way to give every child a turn.

PIECES FOR 1, 2 and 1, 2, 3 BLACK KEYS

Sunshine

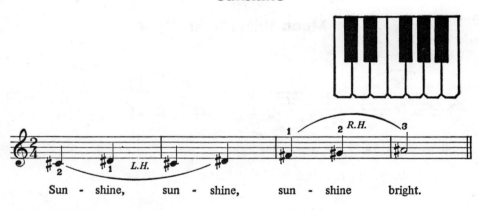

Sun - shine,   sun - shine,   sun - shine   bright.

Motor Skills

- Coordinating left and right fingers to play a melody

Musical Focus

- Hearing, playing, singing five-tone (pentatonic) pieces

Activities and Directions

- Children may stand around keyboard.

- *We play our new piece on a group of <u>two</u> and a group of <u>three</u> black keys.*
- Play "Sunshine" on middle keyboard.
- Sing it. Children repeat it.
- Play it for singing.
- With your back to the children play the left hand (Sunshine, sunshine) in the air or on a chart. Children copy fingers (fingers 2—1) and sing. Check fingering.
- Play right hand (sunshine bright) in the air, children copying (fingers 1—2—3).
- Repeat the entire piece in the air or on chart.
- Play it for singing. Children play it in the air or on desk charts.
- Two children come to keyboard to play with teacher (one on each side). Each finds a set of 1—2 and 1—2—3 to play.
- All play together two or three times.
- Other children take turns at the keyboard.
- *We played a piece called "Sunshine."*

Moon Shines in My Room

Relaxed rhythm

Moon-shines in   my room to - night;   As   I   go   to   sleep.

- Follow the routine for "Sunshine."

Old McDonald Had a Farm

- Children learn the song by rote.
- One child accompanies the "Quack quack's."
- Everyone learns to play "Ei ei oh."
- Everyone learns to play "Old McDonald had a farm."

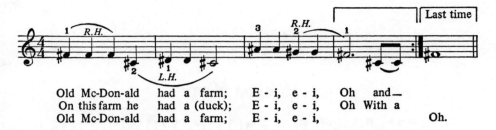

Old Mc-Don-ald had a farm; E - i, e - i, Oh and—
On this farm he had a (duck); E - i, e - i, Oh With a
Old Mc-Don-ald had a farm; E - i, e - i, Oh.

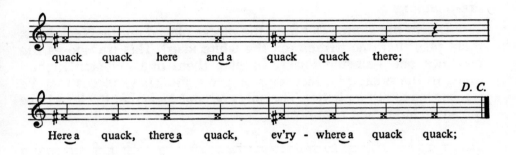

quack quack here and a quack quack there;

Here a quack, there a quack, ev'ry - where a quack quack;

- Children take turns playing parts or all of the song. High and low sets of keys may be used when several children play.

BLACK KEY RECITAL

A recital is a program of pieces. When you play on a recital you must know the piece very well.

Here is a list of pieces to choose from when you select your recital piece:

- *Two Black Keys:* Play Hop Game, Jingles, Marching, Bye Low.
- *Three Black Keys:* Jingles, Walking, Shells and Sand.
- *1, 2, 3 and 1, 2 Black Keys:* Climbing Up the Mountain, Down the Mountain Down.
- *1, 2, and 1, 2, 3 Black Keys:* Sunshine, Moon Shines in My Room, Old McDonald.
- Some pieces may be played by two or more children as an ensemble.

White Keys

TRANSPOSING BLACK KEY PIECES TO WHITE KEYS

Pre-planning

Delete the sharps (#) from the pieces played on the black keys; then, play them as written (on the white keys). This transposes the melodies one half-step lower. To play them one half-step higher, move to the adjacent white keys on the right. These pieces may be transposed to other pitches. The only prerequisite is that the keys have the same intervallic relationship.

March-ing

Motor Skills

- Using familiar finger patterns in new keyboard locations

Musical Skills

- Recognizing aurally one-step intervals
- Transposing by ear familiar melodies originally played on black keys

Activities and Directions

- *We can play "Marching" on black keys (Play on C#—D#) or we can play "Marching" on white keys. (Play on C—D.)*
- A volunteer plays "Marching" as learned on the two black keys. Other children watch the keyboard.
- To a child at the keyboard: *Slide your fingers off the black keys (to the left) to the white keys next to them.* Help the child if necessary. If the children cannot see the keyboard, use a wall chart to show them what was done.
- Have the child play "Marching" on white keys (C—D). Children with desk charts may play along (and sing, too).

- *You played "Marching" on lower keys.*
- Several children play "Marching," first on the black keys then on the white (C—D).
- *We can play "Marching" on higher white keys.*
- Demonstrate by playing "Marching" on the black keys, then moving to the right to play it on D—E. (As before, use the wall chart for demonstration if necessary.)
- Several children play "Marching" on D—E.
- *We played "Marching" three places.*
- **Lesson may end here.**
- *Can we play "Marching" on other keys?*
- Let volunteers briefly explore the possibilities. This sets the stage for later individual exploration.
- End the lesson with someone playing "Marching" first on the black keys, then on other keys.

Continuing Activities

- Make the keyboard available for individual exploration at convenient times.
- Adapt this lesson to transposing "Bye Low" and "Shells and Sand."
- To challenge the able child, adapt this lesson to melodies using all five black keys.

THE STRONG FINGERS
(A mini-story)

Motor Skills

- Choosing matching strong fingers (probably index fingers)
- Eye and finger coordination

Musical Focus

- Review of low, high and middle pitches

Activities and Directions

- *This is a funny story for you to play on the white keys.*

- Choose a *strong* finger on your left hand.
  It sits on the lowest white key.
  Choose the same kind of strong finger on your right hand.
  It sits on the highest white key.
  The two strong fingers would like to meet.
  The left strong finger starts to walk up the keyboard.
  The right strong finger starts to walk down the keyboard.
  The strong fingers meet in the middle of the keyboard.
  And . . . Guess what?
  The strong fingers find out that they are look-alike fingers.
  So they wiggle. And someone giggles.
  Then, the left strong finger walks back down the keyboard.
  And the right strong finger walks back up the keyboard.
  And finally, they are right back where they started.
  The left strong finger sits on the lowest white key.
  The right strong finger sits on the highest white key.

Creative Play at the Keyboard

THE ANIMALS AT THE ZOO
(a mini-story)

Activities and Directions

Playing Positions at the Keyboard	*Beside the Keyboard*
Lion, Elephant, Monkeys, Birds	*Giraffe*

Lion: (Any lowest keys) Push down with two fists.

Elephant: (Black keys below middle C) Alternate fists on two groups.

Monkeys: (White keys above middle C) Alternate left and right fingers in any order to make the chatter.

Birds: (Any highest keys) Alternate two or three keys as fast as possible (trill) like a bird song.

Giraffe: (Blinking) No sound.

- *The animals at the zoo were glad to see me. The lion roared* (keyboard) *and roared* (keyboard). *The elephant rocked back and forth* (keyboard), *back and forth* (keyboard). *The monkeys chattered* (keyboard) *and chattered* (keyboard). *The birds sang* (keyboard) *and sang* (keyboard). *But . . .* (silence) *The Giraffe only blinked.*

- The children may stand around the piano.

- Tell the story at the piano, creating your own sounds (as above), and turning around to blink for the giraffe.

- Discuss the sounds made by each animal, why the giraffe makes no sound (no voice), and how the children might make imitative sounds at the keyboard.

- One at a time, the children experiment with the keyboard sounds. One may be the lion; one, the elephant; one, the monkeys; one, the birds; and one, the giraffe who stands beside the keyboard and blinks.

- Five children stand at the keyboard and play as the teacher or a child tells the story.

185

- *We told the zoo story at the keyboard.*

Continuing Activities

- Relate this activity to "Sounds of Zoo Creatures" (Part 1) and "One Elephant" (Part 1).
- Create keyboard sounds for "The Noisy Giant the Quiet Little Pony" (Part 2) and "The Rain Storm" (Part 2).

♪ ♪ ♪ ♪ ♪

Guided exploration on the keyboard gives children an opportunity, not only to hear the wide range of pitches from very low to very high, but also to see chromatic pitches laid out in an orderly manner. This visual concept of pitch is another link in the chain of music learnings. Children see, play and hear pitches in their singing range and beyond. With keyboard playing, another element of music has been added.

PART 5

Special Activities
& Programs

Part 5

SPECIAL ACTIVITIES AND PROGRAMS

Demonstration Lessons
   Model Demonstration (Clarinet)

Formal Programs for a
   Kindergarten Audience
   Two Model Programs (Piano)

♪ ♪ ♪ ♪ ♪

Although every day is a special day in the lives of kindergarten children, some days are very special. Part 5 contains music for these times. A birthday and the singling out of one child for attention, Halloween and dressing up, Thanksgiving and patriotic holidays with both serious and playful activities, Valentine's Day and being friends, Arbor Day with emphasis on growing things, Mother's Day and Father's Day and the thoughtful attention of children — all these things roll around each year, new every time and every time to be celebrated with music.

There are also songs for the seasons: beginning with fall, when changes in weather are apt to be striking; on to winter with snow or imagined snow; and finally, to spring and new life. Children are very interested in nature's ways and must sing about them. As the school year ends they can sing about the coming summer fun.

Three models for different kinds of marching are included, not only because of children's love of marching, but also because of rhythmic learning that takes place when children march to music.

Children naturally improvise in song and movement and sometimes on simple instruments in order to express their feelings, celebrate a happening or act out a story. Suggestions and models in Part 5 help the teacher guide children in developing their own music.

Musical programs and celebrations in kindergarten are the outcome of day by day musical learning. These programs are opportunities for children to formalize and to share the music they like and perform the best. Suggestions in Part 5 outline the steps in preparing and performing eight model programs.

Not only is it important for children to perform, it is also important for them to be a musical audience, and to listen to skilled performers from whom they can learn. For this reason, lessons in audience etiquette are included. A guide for developing demonstrations of instruments and short formal or informal programs FOR children is provided for musicians who plan programs for kindergarten children.

Songs for Special Days and Times

WHO HAS A BIRTHDAY?

Vigorously

1. Who has a birth - day? Who has a birth - day?
2. (Jim - my) has a birth - day; (Jim - my) has a birth - day;

Who has a birth - day? Clap, Birth - day?
(Jim - my) has a birth - day. Stamp, Birth - day.
                                Drum, etc.

3. Let's count the birthday; Let's count the birthday; (1, 2, 3, 4, - and 5) or (1, 2, 3, 4, -5, 6).
   (Other verses: Let's clap (dance, march, drum,
   eat, etc.)

Materials

- Drum (optional)

Musical Focus

- Accented rhythm

Activities and Directions

- *Someone has a birthday today.*
- Sing the first verse.
- Identify the birthday child.
- Sing verse 2. Have the children join in.
- Count the years in rhythm to prepare for verse 3.

- Sing verse 3. Have the children join in.
- Add other verses.
- Sing the traditional "Happy Birthday" song.
- *We celebrated the birthday with singing.*

ON HALLOWEEN NIGHT
(A musical story)

On Halloween night I saw a big orange moon hanging low in the sky. The moon shone on:

a funny jack-o-lantern who blinked and blinked and
    blinked;
and a little black cat who meowed, me - owed , me -
owed ,
and a scary, white ghost who swished and
    swished and swished.

(Other creatures associated with Halloween may be added with their appropriate sounds.)

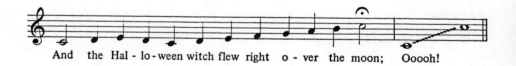

And   the Hal - lo - ween witch flew right   o - ver the moon;   Ooooh!

- *For flannel board* children may make the paper cutouts (orange moon, yellow jack-o-lantern, black cat, white ghost, black witch). As they are mentioned, put figures on the board. Make the witch fly over the moon and disappear.

- *To act out:* Children hold paper cutouts, the bigger the better. As the creatures are mentioned, the children sing the part and form a line. The witch cutout is made to fly over the moon, then the child holding the witch cutout runs away.

CELEBRATE A HAPPY DAY
(Thanksgiving, Hanukah, Christmas)

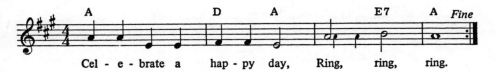

Cel - e - brate a   hap - py day,   Ring,   ring,   ring.

Ring,   ring,   ring,   ring,   Ring - a - ring - a - ring.

Introduction on keyboard or guitar: Play first phrase or A, E7, A chords. Use all available bells on "ring."

- *Thanksgiving* (Resonator bells A, B, A for introduction and "Sing, sing, sing.")

> Celebrate Thanksgiving Day, Sing, sing, sing;
> Celebrate Thanksgiving Day, Sing, sing, sing.
> Thankful for the food we eat and for the clothes we
>   wear;
> Celebrate Thanksgiving Day, Sing, sing, sing.

- *Hanukah* (Tambourines)

> Celebrate for Hanukah, Ching, ching, ching;
> Celebrate for Hanukah, Ching, ching, ching.
> Light the candles, Dance and sing, a-ching-a-ching-
>   a-ching;
> Celebrate for Hanukah, Ching, ching, ching.

- *Christmas* (Jingle bells)

> Celebrate for Christmas Day, Jingle, jing, jing;
> Celebrate for Christmas Day, Jingle, jing, jing,
> Ring the bells for Christmas Day a-jingle, jingle,
>   jing;
> Celebrate for Christmas Day, Jingle, jing, jing.

OH CHRISTMAS TREE
(adapted from the German folk song "O Tannenbaum")

Oh Christ-mas tree, Oh Christ-mas tree;. How love-ly are your branch-es.

You're   al - ways   green   the   whole   year   through;

You're   al - ways   green   the   whole   year through;

Variations for Phrase Three

- While working on ornaments:
1. We're making paper chains for you (repeat).
2. I'm cutting out a star for you (repeat).
3. With brushes and with colored paints we're making orna-ments with paints.
4. I'm working with a chunk of clay to make a Christmas ball today.
5. We'll decorate the Christmas tree (repeat).
    - Add verses created by children.
    - Decorating the tree:
1. Children sit or stand around the tree.
2. On phrase three, sing, "We decorate the Christmas tree (re-peat) while individuals or small groups place their hand-made ornaments on the tree. (This is also a good time for the chil-dren to sing their original phrases.)
3. If this is the beginning activity of a decorating party, the song may end with the children forming a circle and dancing around the tree ("We dance around the Christmas tree") and back to their seats.
    - Encourage children to express themselves by singing these or their original solos:

1. The lights are red and green and blue (repeat).
2. The tree is beautiful to see (repeat).
3. We put our pictures on the tree (repeat).
4. Under the tree the presents wait (repeat).

VALENTINE

(For the children to sing as they create paper valentines using red paper, white paper, paper lace doilies, scissors, and paste.)

Val - en - tine,   val - en - tine;   Will you   be   my   val - en - tine?

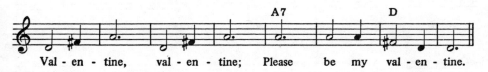

Val - en - tine,   val - en - tine;   Please   be   my   val - en - tine.

Activities and Directions

- *As we make our valentines we will learn a Valentine song.*
- Sing the song.
- *Sing the first part with me.* (First 4 measures)
- *Listen to the next part.* (Measures 5—8) Children repeat it.
- *Sing the next part with me.* (Measures 9—12)
- *Listen to the last part.* (Measures 13—16) Children repeat.
- *Let's sing all of the song together as we work on our Valentines.* (Sing.)

Variations for continuing Valentine activities

- Fit the words into the basic melody:

    1. I am making Valentines; Will you be my Valentine?
       I am making Valentines; Please be my Valentine.
    2. Valentine box of red; etc.
    3. No one knows my Valentine etc.
    4. Can you guess my Valentine? etc.

THE AMERICAN FLAG

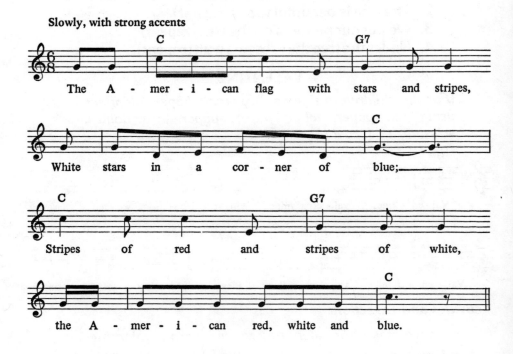

Slowly, with strong accents

The A - mer - i - can flag with stars and stripes,

White stars in a cor - ner of blue;_____

Stripes of red and stripes of white,

the A - mer - i - can red, white and blue.

- In the other verses the words differ only in the first phrase. Adapt the words to the basic rhythm of the song:

  2. On holidays we fly the flag etc.
  3. To begin the day we salute the flag etc.
  4. In a big parade the flag leads the way etc.

Enrichments for Performance

- Drums keep the beat.
- Children march in place as they sing or enter stage singing.
- Children hold paper flags made by them.
- Children look toward the flag as they sing.
- Resonator bells, C and G keep time using chord symbols as a guide.
- Teacher may play chord accompaniment on autoharp, guitar, keyboard or melody accompaniment on recorder, etc.

ARBOR DAY

(In some states Arbor Day is a legal holiday set aside for the planting of trees.)

Part 1. *Growing Like Trees*

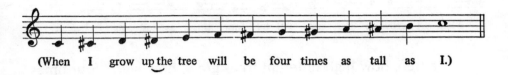

(When   I   grow   up the tree   will   be   four   times   as   tall   as   I.)

Materials

- Mallet bells, keyboard or other chromatic instrument

Musical Focus

- Developing the concept of small intervals—half steps
- Feeling a long ascending musical line

Activities and Directions

- *Trees grow very slowly. Let's find out how slowly we can grow with this music.*
- Play the half step or chromatic scale.
- *Crouch on the floor. Grow slowly so you will be stretching your arms and head at the end of the music.*
- Play the scale again as the children "grow."
- Repeat it several times so that the children will learn to end with the music.
- *Let's grow once more like a tree.*

Part 2. *Arbor Day*

Activities and Directions

- *Arbor Day is the day for planting trees.*
- *Trees grow slowly but they grow taller than people.*
- Sing the song.
- Lead a short discussion of trees near the school, the planting of

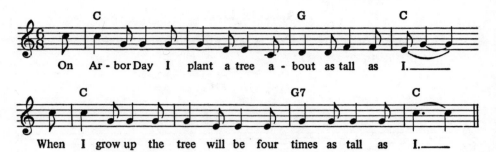

a tree, how high different trees grow, how high "four times"
is.

- Sing the first two measures. Children repeat.
- Continue this phrase by phrase learning.
- *Listen to the whole song.* Sing the song.
- Children sing the song.
- *Let's sing it once more. Then let's grow with the music.* (Repeat "Growing Like Trees.")

Continuing Activity

- If feasible, a tree may be planted in a planter or in the schoolyard. Use the song as a culmination to the planting.

IN HONOR OF MY MOTHER (FATHER)

This song needs no special enrichment although a chordal accompaniment may be used to keep the rhythm and pitch accurate.

The song may be adapted to honor heroes, special visitors or children at special times.

Songs for the Seasons

LEAVES ARE SLOWLY FALLING

2. My hands are out to catch them as they fall.
   My hands are out to catch them as they fall.
   They were green last summer but they're red and
        yellow now;
   My hands are out to catch them as they fall.
3. The wind is blowing, blowing leaves to me.
4. Now all the leaves have fallen from the trees.
5. The branches of the trees are bare and brown.
6. My feet are crackling through the fallen leaves.

Materials

- (Optional) Real or paper leaves colored by the children

Musical Focus

- Sequencing verses in ballad style

Activities and Directions

- *In autumn the weather is cool and the leaves turn to red and yellow.*
- Sing the song.
- Children show leaves they have collected or paper leaves they have colored. In the discussion the children demonstrate how the leaves fall from the trees.

- Sing verse once again with the children.
- Sing through the other verses with children repeating each verse.
- Repeat the entire song with children indicating the action in their own way, perhaps with leaves.
- *We sang about the falling leaves and the wind in the autumn.*

SNOWFLAKES

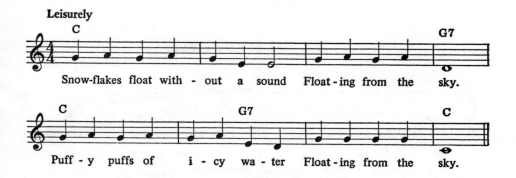

2. Snowflakes on my nose and lips, On my lashes, too;
   On my mittens, cap and coat, Covering my shoes.
3. Moving like a puffy flake, Making not a sound;
   Hands move left and hands move right, Floating, floating down.
4. When the snow is on the ground, I crunch it with my feet;
   Walking, crunching, running, crunching; Crunching with my feet.

Activities and Directions

- *In winter it is cold and sometimes it snows.* (The day of the first snow is a good time to introduce this song.)
- Sing the song.
- Discuss what snow is; watch it from the window; tell about experiences in the snow; etc.
- Sing the song with the children, showing how snowflakes float down.

- Sing verse 2. When the children repeat it, they point to nose, etc., when mentioned in the song.
- *Our song was about snowflakes in winter.*

Continuing

- Add verses 3 and 4 and use the song for rhythmic movement and acting out. Emphasize the sequence of happenings.
- Through a magnifying glass look at snowflakes on a piece of wool or velvet. Make up a new verse about how the snow-flakes looked magnified.

IN THE SPRINGTIME

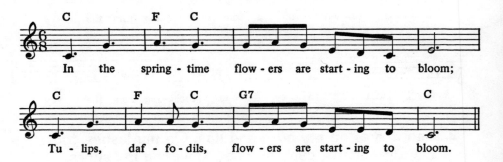

2. In the springtime I hear the rain on the roof;
   Pit, pat, pit, pat; I hear the rain on the roof.
3. In the springtime I hear the little birds sing;
   Tweet, tweet, tweet, tweet; I hear the little birds sing.
4. In the springtime bunnies are hopping around;
   Hop, hop, hop, hop; bunnies are hopping around.
5. In the springtime chickens are fluffy and soft;
   Cheep, cheep, cheep, cheep; chickens are fluffy and soft.

Materials

- (Optional) Flowers or pictures of things mentioned in the song

Musical Focus

- Free and imitative expression

Activities and Directions

- *In the springtime it begins to get warmer and the flowers bloom.*
- Sing the song.
- Discuss tulips, daffodils. Show pictures, if flowers are not available.
- Sing the song again with the children.
- *What other things make you think of spring?*
- Use this question-answer period to lead into some of the other verses (or original verses).
- *We sang about spring.*

HOT IN THE SUMMERTIME

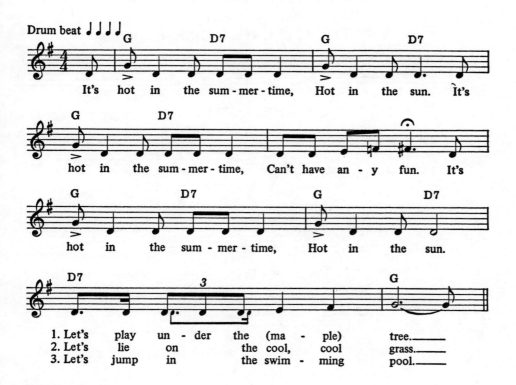

Materials

- Drum

Musical Focus

- Strong, even beat (rock) and syncopation

Activities and Directions

- *This song makes us think of a day when it's too hot to play.*
- Sing the song, playing a strong accent on the drum.
- Discuss hot weather, sun and shade, kinds of play for hot weather.
- Sing the song again with children joining in.
- *Can you think of other ways to keep cool on a hot summer day?*
- Incorporate suggestions into the last phrase of the song or sing verse two or three. Volunteers keep the beat on the drum.
- *Let's clap* (stamp, move upper body) *as we sing with the drum.*

EV'RY THING IS GREEN, GREEN, GREEN

2. Ev'ry thing is blue, blue, blue.
The sky is blue, and eyes are blue;
Sometimes I like to paint with blue.
The sky is blue and eyes are blue;
Ev'ry thing is blue, blue, blue.

3. Ev'ry thing is red, red, red.
The leaves are red and berries red;
I'm putting on my red, red cap;
The leaves are red, and berries red;
Ev'ry thing is red, red, red.

4. Ev'ry thing is white, white, white.
The snow is white and bears are white;
Sometimes my socks and shirts are too;
The snow is white and bears are white;
Ev'ry thing is white, white, white.

Activities and Directions

- *In the springtime the grass and the trees turn green again.*
  In the summertime the sky is very blue.
  In autumn some leaves turn red.
  In winter it snows.
- Sing the song, acting out holding the leaves.
- Talk about the grass and trees near the school.
- All sing the song.
- Suggest finding all the green things in the room, an art session painting leaves, or a leaf-gathering walk.
- All sing the song again.
- *We sang about green (_____) and green (_____).*

Songs for Marching

PAT-A-PAT-A-PAN
(Marching and Drumming)
(Review Lesson "Pat the Drum Box")

Slow Accented

Burgundian Carol

I will play up-on my drum with a pat-a-pat-a-pan; I will play up-on my drum, pat-a-pat-a-pan, pat-a-pat-a-pan. I will play up-on my drum with a pat-a-pat-a-pan.

Informal Use with Keyboard or Other Accompaniment

- Have the children take turns keeping time on available drums until all have had a turn.
- Use it for a stand-still march with children keeping time with feet, arms, head and upper body.
- Use it for a "Follow the Drummer" march. Children march single-file behind the drummer-leader.
- After a drum making-decorating session children will enjoy it as a "show-off" piece.

Activities and Directions

Part 1

- *One hand is a drum. The other hand is a patter.*
- *Like this.* Demonstrate. Hold one hand flat. The fingers of the other hand pat the flat palm.
- *My hands call you with a "pat-a-pat-a-pan" and your hands answer "pat-a-pat-a-pan."*
- Sing the call-answer pattern several times as you check the patting technique. This will familiarize the children with the melody.
- *Now we're ready. My call* (voice-hands) *and your answer.* For some children the finger patting may involve a new, fine coordination pattern.
- Repeat several ways. Children call-teacher answer. Groups call and answer. One hand on call. Change to other hand for answer. A few children may be ready for partner call and answer.
- *I will sing our new drum song. Listen for the call and answer part. Raise your hand when you hear it.* Sing. (Some children may point out the slow patterns.)
- Sing the song with the children playing the call-answer.
- *We played call-answer with pat-a-pat-a-pan.*
- The lesson may be extended to include the playing on one or two drums.

Part 2

- *Let's sing and play our call-answer pat-a-pat-a-pan.*
- Review the song with children taking turns playing the patterns on a hand drum.
- *Are there other pat-a-pat-a-pan's in the song?* (two others)
- *Are they slow or are they fast like the call-answer?* (slow and different)
- Sing the first phrase patting the first slow pat-a-pat-a-pan. Sing this several times with the children.
- Sing the last phrase several times with the children.

- All sing and pat the new pattern. Volunteers may play it on a drum.
- Sing the whole song with drummers playing all the pat-a-pat-a-pan patterns.
- *This song has slow and fast "Pat-a-pat-a-pan's."*

Continuing Activities

- To program the song, set a pattern then rehearse it the same way each time.

Variations:

1. Enter: march, sing and drum
   All sing and hand-pat.
   Exit: march, sing and drum
2. Introduction: Call-answer by drummers.
   All sing with drummers playing the 4 patterns.
   All sing with hand-patting.
   All sing. Some hand-pat, others drum.
3. Introduction on keyboard (Play first phrase.)
   All sing and hand-pat.
   Repeat with drummers accompanying with call-answer pattern all the way through (Challenging.)

THE SPECIAL BAND

Materials

- Instruments to be used (10, 7, or 4)

Musical Focus

- Playing instruments on cue
- Beginning ensemble performance

This song provides an opportunity to use all available instruments—drums, jingle bells, triangle, and cymbals (plus the resonator bell C). It gives a chance for independent use of playing techniques developed in earlier, more specialized lessons. To keep instruments silent but ready to play, children hold them in their lap.

Slow March
Well accented

Traditional

There was 1, There were 2, There were 3 lit - tle chil - dren.

There were 4, There were 5, There were 6 lit - tle chil - dren.

There were 7, There were 8, There were 9 lit - tle chil - dren.

10 lit - tle chil - dren in the band.

Chorus: Was - n't that a band in the morn - ing, in the morn - ing, in the morn - ing? Was - n't that a band in the morn - ing, in the ear - ly morn?

This song is traditionally for ten children, each playing an instrument. However, it may include a larger number by inserting numbers between measures 12 and 13. To use seven children begin measure 4, count 2 and sing, "There was one," etc. To use four children begin measure 8, count 2 and adapt the numbers.

Each child has a number and an instrument (or a pretend instrument) and plays when his/her number is sung. For further individual identification each child may stand to play. Everyone plays on the chorus. As an informal activity children may sit in a circle and pass the instruments to the next person on repeats. A challenging variation is to sing the verse backwards starting with "ten." All players drop out after their numbers are sung. Number one ends the song.

Introductory Lessons

1. Start with the chorus. Use clapping or finger patting. Add one instrument (to be used later in the verse) on each repeat until all instruments are being played. Check holding and playing techniques. Repeat this with new sets of children until all have participated. After the chorus is familiar proceed to the verse.
2. Introduce the verse, emphasizing the counting. Number the children. Repeat several times with each child standing on his/her number to set the counting pattern. Give each numbered child an instrument. Repeat the verse with children playing the instruments on their numbers. Add the chorus with everyone playing the beat.

POLYRHYTHM PARADE
(Name Walk)

Focus

- Walking rhythms

Activities and Directions

The First Time
- *Each one of you has a different name. You can walk in time to your name.*
- *I'm walking to my name* (teacher's name, teacher's name). Walk across the room and back, whispering your name and keeping time.
- Call on a child to do the same using his/her name.
- Other children try it.
- *Each one of you had a different walk.*

Developing an Informal Parade (Especially good for the playground)

- One at a time each child says, "I'm walking to my name (Johnny Jones, Johnny Jones,)" then goes anywhere on the playground whispering his/her name and keeping time. This continues until all have taken off on the name walk. The children may walk until they tire of the game or until the teacher signals that the game is over.

Developing a Formal Parade

- Establish a parade route for a single-file parade, i.e., around the room, around tables, and finally back to the beginning of the parade route.
- Choose a leader (or be the leader yourself).
- All line up at the beginning of the route.
- The leader speaks his/her name (Johnny Jones, Johnny Jones) and starts walking to his/her rhythm, whispering the name as he/she walks. As soon as the first child starts whispering, the second child announces his/her name and follows whispering his/her name. This continues until all are walking and whispering and finish the parade route.
- *All the name-whispering together made a buzzing sound. Your feet made many different rhythms.*

As the Beginning of a Performance (Children entering on stage)

- The leader announces his/her name, then walks and whispers as he/she proceeds to the assigned place. Others quickly follow.
- This introduces each child and also set the stage formation for the first number on the program.

Improvisational Performances

Spontaneous musical performances may seem to spring entirely from the imagination of children. However, when kindergarten children improvise, they use not only their imaginations but also their previous musical experiences, especially informal, teacher-guided involvements. Important to successful improvisation is their growing understanding of basic musical concepts such as loud-soft, high-low, fast-slow, even-uneven rhythms, and timbre.

As a result of their experimentation they begin to analyze musical elements in their own way. Early improvisational performances may be so extemporaneous that only those involved are aware of the performance. If the performers are satisfied, the objectives have been met.

Later improvisations, especially those involving groups working within a picture or story framework, may be repeated many times with possible variations. Remembered improvisational performances may become the basis for more ambitious stage-oriented projects. Remarks such as these are evidence of children's analytical development: "This is a loud song." "I'm dancing fast." "That bird sang high." "Sh! I'm in between the music." "Those cymbals made me jump." "I sang low when I fell down."

With a preliminary background of information, guided experimentation, and modeled experiences, children gradually extend their activities and synthesize musical elements into new and original arrangements. Their achievements are kindergarten improvisation in its finest form. The children are using what they know and feel to create music.

Many earlier lessons in this book have emphasized exploratory improvisation in movement, sound, form, sequencing, and dramatic play. The following models in guided improvisation are extensions of those lessons.

♪ ♪ ♪ ♪ ♪

THE WIND AND THE LEAVES
(A companion to "The Leaves Are Softly Falling")

The Experience

- A walk through autumn leaves, listening to the sound of leaves crackling underfoot, watching the leaves flutter, drift, and fall

The Improvisation (Letters indicate new or repeated actions.)

A. Children are walking through the dry leaves (crushing tissue paper; making mouth or hand sounds—the result of experimentation).

B. Leaves still on the tree flutter in the breeze (sighing sounds, shaking movement or other original suggestions).

A. Children are still walking around the tree. (A walking rhythm is probably beginning to emerge.)

C. A few leaves let go of the tree and slowly drift downward (whole body movement, no sound).

A. Children still walking.

C. More leaves fall.

A. Children still walking.

D. A heavy gust of wind makes all the leaves shudder, then drift rhythmically down to the ground.

A. Children run through the leaves catching the newly fallen leaves and moving away from the barren tree.

Further Developments for Programming

- Children choose to be the tree, the breeze, the wind, etc.
- The action may precede the song, "The Leaves Are Softly Falling," then follow the song as the children leave the scene.
- Sound makers (rubbing drum heads, tapping wood blocks or sticks) may be added to the performance.

HEAR ME PLAY
Companion to "The Special Band" (Part 5)

Traditional French March—"The King of France"

Accompaniment pattern

Experience

- Exploring different classroom instruments in activities (Parts 2, 3, 4)

Improvisation

- Children choose their instruments (or teacher distributes them).
- Sing, *Hear me play; I play the big piano* (I play upon the organ); *Hear me play; I play the big piano.*
- Play through the piece without singing.
- *You all have special instruments to play. Who has a (drum)?*
- (To the drummer) *You sing "Hear me play; I play upon my drum, etc." Then you play and sing it again.*
- The drummer(s) play and sing.
- Other children sing and play their instruments (all drums, all jingle bells).
- After all have played individually: *Let's all play our special pieces together. This time we will not sing. Keep time with the (piano).*

- *The music was good for one instrument and for all our instruments.*
- If only part of the children have played the instruments, repeat the lesson with another group of children.

Suggestions for Programming

- Preparation: All children have instruments which may be commercial, children or teacher made, or improvised materials such as keys, clapping shoes together, slapping a table or book. Listen to each instrument. Then divide the sounds into groups with similar timbre (jingles, drum-like, clicking, rattling, etc.).
- Performance: Play the march on the piano or other keyboard.
- Each player in one group plays a short solo.
- The group plays with the piano.
- Repeat with every group.
- End with all children playing together.

Some Suggested Verses

"Hear me play; I play upon my drum." (The jingles bells a-jingle; I'm shaking the maracas; the woodblock keeps the beat.)

THE SPIDER ON THE CEILING

Experience

- Watching a spider; learning facts about spiders
- "Tip Toddle" (Part 1) or an original quiet dance

Improvisation

- A finger drum or rhythm sticks may accompany the developing drama.
- This rhyme or the children's description of the spider aims to begin the imitative play and set up a rhythm.

"A spider's on the ceiling and his eyes are looking
    down.
He sees the children dancing; they're dancing all
    around.
Children   dancing,   dancing; Children   dancing
    'round."

- Children dance and sing ("Tip Toddle"). As they continue
  their dancing they look up and gradually spread out, leaving
  an empty space in the middle of the group.

"The spider's spinning, spinning, a long, long thread.
Then, Down he zooms, down; On the long, long
    thread."

- The children scatter and leave the spider in the middle.
- (The improvisation may end here.)
- Guide the action, chanting, singing and dancing with questions such as these: *What do the children do after the spider
  is on the floor? Do they watch the spider? Dance around the
  spider? What does the spider do? Does the spider dance?*
- Use the children's improvisations for the ending.

Musical Programs and Celebrations
by Children

Musical performances and celebrations by kindergarten children may be informal—prepared for their own satisfaction without an audience or for a small peer group or a gathering of parents. They may also be formal exhibitions of the children's musical abilities staged for an audience.

In either case the performances are the culmination of musical learning experiences involving one or more facets of the music program. Performances may be achieved through improvisation or directed learning and memorization. When the children know a few songs, dances, dramatizations, or other musical numbers, they are ready for a review. This is a good time for children to entertain themselves with a little program. The thing that makes such a program special is that all of the music is well learned by all.

PREPARING FOR A MUSICAL PROGRAM

Select material for a program from music the children like best, music they perform well, and that is appropriate for the occasion. There should be a variety of music with some contrast. Include several kinds of activities—chanting and/or singing, instrument playing, and physical interpretations (dancing, hand patterns or gestures).

After the music has been chosen, include it in daily music sessions so that it becomes very familiar. Whenever possible, use improvisations created by the children.

Before a formal program, especially in a place other than the classroom, arrange a short rehearsal. If this is not possible, simulate the place in the classroom. The goal of the performance is personal satisfaction in achieving musical excellence; that is, performing to the best of their ability.

MODEL PROGRAMS

The following program suggestions are made up of material from all parts of the book, (Each piece is labeled with the part from

219

which it comes—1, 2, 3, 4, 5.) The programs are short with the time determined somewhat by the amount of improvisation and other enrichment involved.

Each program focuses on a central theme and includes a variety of musical activities. These model programs illustrate the flexibility possible in developing performances by kindergarten children. Other music may be substituted or added.

Autumn

- My Year (2) (Autumn verse)
- The Wind and the Leaves (5) and/or
  Leaves Are Slowly Falling (5)
- The Rain Storm (2)
- (Optional) One of the following or other familiar song: On Halloween Night (5), Skip to My Lou (1), Listen to the Clock (1), A Giant Man Dances (1)
- The School Bells and Little Mattie (3)

It's Wintertime

- Pat-a-Pat-a-Pan (5)
- The Jingle Drum (2)
- Oh Christmas Tree (5) or The Snow Is Dancing (1)
- Selected Keyboard Pieces (4)
- Jingle Bell Ride (3)

Celebration of Spring

- Chant of the Seasons (1) (Spring verse)
- Bird Rondo (1)
- Let It Grow (1)
- The Noisy Giant and the Quiet Little Pony (2) or Dancing to Music (3)
- In the Springtime (5)

Summer (End of School)

- Polyrhythm March (5) (Entrance)
- Swinging in a Hammock (3)

- The Bug Story (1) or Hear the Mosquito (1)
- Japanese Rain Song (1) or Shells and Sand, Sunshine, Moon Shines in My Room (4)
- Hot in the Summertime (5)

Patriotic Program

- Stars and Stripes Forever (Entrance) (1)
- In Honor of (   ) (version improvised for the occasion)
- Flim Flam (2) and/or I'm a Drum, Drum, Drummer (2)
- Hear Them Ring (3) or Celebrate a Happy Day (5)
- The American Flag (5)

Soft and Loud Sounds

- Choose from these listings. Alternate soft and loud pieces.

Soft Sounds	Loud Sounds
Hear the Mosquito (1)	Galloping (1)
It Sings Up to the Sky (1)	Bong, Bang, Bing (2)
Listen, Listen to the Clock (1)	To Strike a Cymbal (2)
Tip Toddle (1)	Rain Storm (2)
Tiny Toes That Tap (3)	I'm a Drum, Drum,
Jingles and Tingles (3)	Drummer (2)
The First Star Is Lucky (3)	Bang Goes the Drummer (2)
	Rumble Grumble Music (4)

Large and Small Creatures

- One Elephant (1)
- Hear the Mosquito (1) or The Flight of the Bumble Bee (1)
- I Can Stretch Myself (1)
- The Goldfish (1)
- The Animals at the Zoo (4)

A Variety Program

A first experience program may be patterned after this one. Such a program will include whatever activities the children are able to perform.

- Everything is Green, Green, Green (5) (All or the verse for the current season)
- I Can Stretch Myself (1)
  Chug-a-Chug (2) and/or Honey Bear (3)
- The Old Lady and the Drummer Boys (2)

Musical Demonstrations and Programs for Children

KINDERGARTEN CHILDREN AS AN AUDIENCE

All performances for children, whether they are formal programs on a stage or informal demonstrations in a classroom, have certain things in common.

- The length of the program coincides with the attention span of the children. (A program may vary from ten to thirty minutes.)
- Children enjoy a twenty-minute program made up of four or five short pieces better than one twenty-minute piece.
- The children are comfortable with a sense of well-being. They are relaxed because they have been to the rest room, have adjusted any uncomfortable clothing (like untied shoelaces), have just completed a short walk or other mild form of activity, and are ready to sit for a while.
- The children are prepared for what they are to hear. They are expecting music of a certain kind. Their attitude is one of positive expectancy.
- All the children can see and hear the performer(s). They are sitting comfortably and do not have to strain to look up at the performer.
- The children know that they are expected to remain quiet.
- The teacher leads the "thank you" clapping at the proper time.
- The children are actively involved in some way. Participation may range from experimenting with an instrument in a skill demonstration in an informal setting to unison clapping at a formal program.
- Brief explanations, questions and descriptions preceding each piece generally help the children enjoy and understand the music better and also establish a closer rapport between performer and audience.

223

The kindergarten audience is a learning audience. Good musical programs match the ability of the children to understand the music. Both the musical content and its presentation should reinforce the basic concepts of music which the children are currently developing. Clear melodies, decided rhythms, or relaxed rhythms to establish a mood or to portray a setting are important. Compositions with repetition give children an opportunity to absorb phrase structure and content. Both consonant (tonic-dominant) and dissonant sound combinations should be included. At this age most children are still unbiased in their liking for harmony and benefit from hearing many kinds of harmonies.

Different styles of music, music for various instrumental and vocal solo and ensembles, music from the past as well as the present, and familiar and new music are all important to consider when planning a program for a kindergarten audience.

DEMONSTRATION LESSONS
(Program-Lessons)

Demonstrations of various ways to produce musical sounds as yet unfamiliar to kindergarten children are valuable educational experiences. A demonstration may be in a formal setting like an auditorium where the audience is large or it may be in the classroom with the children seated close to the performer-demonstrator. In an auditorium setting, the performance may involve an ensemble such as a band or orchestra. A demonstration in a classroom is more likely to be a solo instrument.

A demonstration lesson may focus on an ensemble, a band or orchestra instrument, piano, guitar or other solo instrument, an informal instrument such as a kazoo or hummer, handmade music makers like a horn made from a hose or a monochord made from a box and string, an ethnic instrument, a vocal skill such as whistling, singing or yodeling, a dance or other rhythmic movement, or any other means of producing basic melody, harmony or rhythm.

A performer-demonstrator may also teach the children how to do what he/she does, as in a demonstration of whistling. The performer may, in some instances, include the classroom percussion instruments in conjunction with the demonstration.

However, the primary purpose of a demonstration lesson is not to teach the children to reproduce the performance, but to introduce them to new ways of performing music, to broaden their understanding of music and to arouse their interest in different kinds of music.

When the lesson is over, the children should know (1) the name of the instrument or skill, (2) what it looks like and sounds like so they could recognize it if they saw or heard it again, (3) basically, how it is played or performed. Finally, they should have some relevant association with the experience.

The following model lesson will establish further guidelines for planning any kinds of demonstration lessons practical for your kindergarten.

AN INSTRUMENTAL DEMONSTRATION
(The Clarinet)

Activities and Directions

- Announce the name of the musical medium. *This is a clarinet. I play it by blowing.* (Drawing the bow across the strings; plucking the strings; striking the metal bars; etc.) Demonstrate briefly.
- Play a short piece. Expect applause and acknowledge it. (Optional: This may precede any announcement and begin the demonstration.)
- *This is the lowest sound I can make.* Demonstrate. (See "Rumble Grumble Music" in Part 4.) *What does it sound like?* Short discussion.
- *This is the highest sound I can make.* Demonstrate. (See "Squeak and Eek Music" in Part 4.) *What does it sound like?* Short discussion.
- *I can make the sound higher or lower by opening and closing the holes.* (putting my fingers on the strings, etc.)
- *Watch my fingers as I make the melody go higher.* Play up the scale. *Where did the melody go?* (Higher)
- *Watch my fingers as I make the melody go lower.* Play down the scale. *Where did the melody go?* (Lower)
- *Listen to this melody called "This Is the Way."* Play it through once.

THIS IS THE WAY

Traditional Tune for
"Here We Go 'Round the Mulberry Bush"

This is the way we clap our hands; Clap our hands, clap our hands,

This is the way we clap our hands, To keep the time of the mu - sic.

- *I need some clappers to keep time.* Play it with children clapping.
- *I need some knee slappers.* Play it with children slapping knees.
- *I need some finger snappers.* Play it with children snapping fingers. (This may be difficult for some children.)
- *I need some singers. Here are the words, "This is the way we sing a song, etc."* Play for the singing.
- *Let's sing "This is the way we clap our hands, etc."* Play for the singing. Repeat any or all the hand actions with words.
- *Listen as I play a piece for you.* Play the same piece as before or another short piece. Expect and acknowledge applause. Indicate that the performance is over.

FORMAL PROGRAMS FOR A KINDERGARTEN AUDIENCE

Attendance of kindergarten children at a formal musical program is a very special occasion. It is a look into the adult world on a kindergarten level. Attending a program in the classroom or school auditorium is actually a preparation for attending a performance in a public concert hall.

A program planned especially for children will consist of several contrasting pieces. The performer will probably introduce each piece with a short explanation, story, or a reference to something familiar to the children. However, the performer may choose to make no explanation but let the music speak for itself. If children are particularly attracted to one piece, it may be repeated. The performer's stage deportment should be friendly but formal, with proper acknowledgment of audience applause, etc.

FOUR MODEL PROGRAMS
(Piano)

The following piano programs are models. Other kinds of musical programs for kindergarten children may follow the same general plan. All programs are thirty minutes or less in length. The music is of average difficulty and can be performed by pianists on the intermediate level. Music has been chosen from 18th, 19th and 20th century piano literature. Further variety has been achieved by including music of contrasting moods and styles, as well as rhythms and keys. Suggested explanations and dialogue follow each program listing.

One of the following numbers may be added to the program or substituted for the last piece listed.

- A song from the children's repertoire (Children may sing with the piano.)
- A recent popular song
- An improvisation on a familiar folk song such as "Old McDonald" or "Oh Susanna"
- A standard ragtime, dixieland, jazz or rock piece
- Any short lively piece in the performer's repertoire

In the last fifty years American composers have taken the lead in composing good piano music for children. One piece on each program is by an American composer. These are representative but may be replaced by similar pieces by American composers in the performers repertoire.

Activities and Directions

Program I.

Theme and Variation *from "Sonata in A Major" (K 300) by Wolfgang Mozart*

Play first eight measures of the theme, first eight measures of variation II, then back to the first eight measures of the theme. For an audience of children with a long attention span, play all the theme and all of variation II. Return to the theme is optional.

- Play the theme.
- *I call this melody a theme. Can you say, "theme"?* (Wait for group response.)
- *When I play the theme again it is a little different. I call this a variation. Can you say, "variation"?* (Wait for response. Prepare to play.)
- *When I finish the theme I will nod my head. Then you will know I am going to play the variation. When the variation is over, I will play the theme again. Listen carefully so you will recognize it.* (Play. Don't forget to nod. A slight breath-like pause will further emphasize the transition.)

Hobby Horse *from "The Album for the Young" Opus 39, no. 3 by Peter I. Tschaikovsky*

- *When you ride your hobby horse you go as fast as you can—just like this piece. Listen.*

Ditty *(A little tune repeated) from "Album for the Young," Op. 68, no. 3 by Robert Schumann.*

- Play the first four measures.
- Play the fragment below, singing as you play. Ask the children to sing it with you. (Repeat)
- As I play the piece you will hear the little song more than once. (The melody occurs six times.)

We can sing this mel-o-dy   loo loo loo loo   loo loo loo loo   loo.

White-Note Clusters, High and Low *from "32 Piano Games" by Ross lee Finney*

- *These are some things for you to listen for in this piece:*
  Low notes (Play.), high notes (Play.).
  Are these notes low or high! (Play low.) Are these notes low
  or high? (Play high.)
- Play first count (crush CDE). *Do you hear one note* (Raise one
  finger.) *or more notes?* (Raise three fingers.) *If you hear one
  note raise one finger. If you hear more notes raise more fin-
  gers.* (Repeat count one.)
- *As I play remember to listen for low notes and high notes.*
- Play.

Game of Tag *from "For Children" vol. II, no. 20 by Bela Bartok*

- *Do you ever play tag?* (Pause for expected response.)
- *When you play tag you run after your friend. When you catch
  him/her, you tag him/her. This piece is about playing tag. I
  wonder if somebody gets tagged. Listen.*

The Clown *from "24 Little pieces" Op. 39 by Dmitri
Kabalewsky*

- *Clowns are funny. They walk around and try to make us laugh.
  I think the clown falls down at the end of this piece. What do
  you think?* (Without waiting for a reply play the piece.)

Program II.

Minuet in G Major *from the "Note-Book of Anna Magdalena
Bach" Johann Sebastian Bach*

- *A minuet makes you want to keep time. Listen to this minuet
  and then tell me how you would like to keep time.*
- Play first sixteen measures. (If this group has a long attention
  span, play all of piece.)
- Children verbalize about how to keep time.
- Invite them to keep time as you play it again.

Fröhlicher Landmann (The Merry Farmer) *from "The Album
for the Young," Op. 68 no. 10 by Robert Schumann*

- *This piece has a low melody which I play with my left hand. Listen,* (Play l.h. first four measures.)
- *My right hand plays "pah pah" like this.* (Demonstrate.)
- *Together they sound like this.* (Play four measures, both hands.)
- *This piece is called "The Merry Farmer." I think this is a very happy kind of piece. Listen.* (Play entire piece.)
- Listen to the comments of the children. If there is time, play the piece again, inviting the children to hum along.

Echoes *from "Suite for the Young" no. 6 by Norman Dello Joio*

- *This piece is called "Echo." When I call to you in a loud voice, "Hello" and you answer me in a soft voice* (indicate their participation.) *"Hello," you are the echo.*
- *When you call "Hello" in a loud voice* (Indicate their participation.) *and I answer you in a soft voice "Hello," I am the echo.*
- *Listen for the loud sounds* (Play measure 1.) *and the soft sounds* (Play measure 2.).
- Play the entire piece.

Touches Blanches *(White Keys) by Darius Milhaud.*

Touches Noire *(Black Keys) by Darius Milhaud.*

(These two pieces are a pair.)

- White Keys.
  - *This piece is played only on the white keys. It is like a dance and moves along, 1, 2, 3.* (Play first four measures and count.) *Watch my fingers and you will see that I play only on the white keys.* (Play entire piece.)
- Black Keys
  - *This piece is a walking piece. Walk and walk and walk and walk.* (Play first four measures as you speak.) *Watch my fingers as they walk on the black keys.*
  - Invite one child to play some walking music on high black keys as you repeat the piece.

♪ ♪ ♪ ♪ ♪

In kindergarten the teacher provides many simple musical experiences—exploration of environmental and musical sounds, directed and free rhythmic movement, chants, songs, much playing of several percussion instruments and limited but musical use of melodic instruments such as bells and keyboard. All these experiences become a musical reservoir from which children draw when they improvise music of their own. Through these varied musical experiences children develop basic concepts of music—the foundation for all music study.

Index